Mobility & Politics

Series editors: **Martin Geiger** (Carleton University, Ottawa, CAN), **Parvati Raghuram** (Open University, Milton Keynes, UK) and **William Walters** (Carleton University, Ottawa, CAN)

Global Advisory Board: Michael Collyer, University of Sussex, Brighton (UK); Susan B. Coutin, University of California, Irvine (US); Raúl Delgado Wise, Universidad Autónoma de Zacatecas, Zacatecas (MEX); Nicholas De Genova, King's College, London (UK); Eleonore Kofman, Middlesex University, London (UK); Rey Koslowski, University at Albany, State University of New York (US); Loren B. Landau, University of the Witwatersrand, Johannesburg (ZA); Sandro Mezzadra,Universitá di Bologna, Bologna (IT); Alison Mountz, Wilfrid Laurier University, Waterloo (CAN); Brett Neilson, University of Western Sydney, Sydney (AUS); Antoine Pécoud, Université Paris 13, Villetaneuse (F); Ranabir Samaddar, Mahanirban Calcutta Research Group, Calcutta (IN); Nandita Sharma, University of Hawai'i at Manoa, Honolulu (US); Tesfaye Tafesse, Addis Ababa University, Addis Ababa (ET); Thanh-Dam Truong, Erasmus University, Rotterdam (NL).

Human mobility, whatever its scale, is often controversial. Hence it carries with it the potential for politics. A core feature of mobility politics is the tension between the desire to maximize the social and economic benefits of migration, and pressures to restrict movement. Transnational communities, global instability, advances in transportation and communication, and concepts of 'smart borders' and 'migration management' are just a few of the phenomena transforming the landscape of migration today. The tension between openness and restriction raises important questions about how different types of policies and politics come to life and influence mobility.

Mobility & Politics invites original, theoretically and empirically informed studies for academic and policy-oriented debates. Authors examine issues such as refugees and displacement, migration and citizenship, security and cross-border movements, (post-)colonialism and mobility, and transnational movements and cosmopolitics.

Other Titles include:

Tanya Basok, Danièle Bélanger, Martha Luz Rojas Wiesner and Guillermo Candiz
RETHINKING TRANSIT MIGRATION
Precarity, Mobility, and Self-Making in Mexico

Liz Montegary and Melissa Autumn White
MOBILE DESIRES
The Politics and Erotics of Mobility Justice

Vicki Squire
POST/HUMANITARIAN BORDER POLITICS BETWEEN MEXICO AND THE US
People, Places, Things

Antoine Pécoud
DEPOLITICISING MIGRATION
Global Governance and International Migration Narratives

Nicos Trimikliniotis, Dimitris Parsanoglou and Vassilis Tsianos
MOBILE COMMONS, MIGRANT DIGITALITIES AND THE RIGHT TO THE CITY

Chris Rumford
COSMOPOLITAN BORDERS

DOI: 10.1057/9781137444646.0001

Also by Suvendrini Perera

REACHES OF EMPIRE: The English Novel from Edgeworth to Dickens

ASIAN AND PACIFIC INSCRIPTIONS: Identities/Ethnicities/Nationalities (*ed.*)

OUR PATCH: Enacting Australian Sovereignty Post-2001 (*ed.*)

AUSTRALIA AND THE INSULAR IMAGINATION: Beaches, Borders, Boats and Bodies

Mobility & Politics

Series Standing Order ISBN 978-1-137-34594-3   hardback
(outside North America only)

You can receive future titles in this series as they are published by placing a standing order. Please contact your bookseller or, in case of difficulty, write to us at the address below with your name and address, the title of the series and the ISBN quoted above.

Customer Services Department, Macmillan Distribution Ltd, Houndmills, Basingstoke, Hampshire RG21 6XS, England

palgrave▶**pivot**

▶

Survival Media: The Politics and Poetics of Mobility and the War in Sri Lanka

Suvendrini Perera

Professor of Cultural Analysis, Curtin University, Australia

DOI: 10.1057/9781137444646.0001

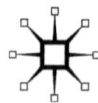

First published in 2016 by

PALGRAVE MACMILLAN® in the United States—a division of St. Martin's Press LLC, 175 Fifth Avenue, New York, NY 10010.

Where this book is distributed in the UK, Europe and the rest of the world, this is by Palgrave Macmillan, a division of Macmillan Publishers Limited, registered in England, company number 785998, of Houndmills, Basingstoke, Hampshire RG21 6XS.

Palgrave Macmillan is the global academic imprint of the above companies and has companies and representatives throughout the world.

Palgrave® and Macmillan® are registered trademarks in the United States, the United Kingdom, Europe and other countries.

ISBN: 978-1-137-44463-9 Hardback
ISBN: 978-1-137-44465-3 EPUB
ISBN: 978-1-137-44464-6 PDF

Library of Congress Cataloging-in-Publication Data is available from the Library of Congress.

A catalogue record of the book is available from the British Library.

First edition: 2016

www.palgrave.com/pivot

DOI: 10.1057/9781137444646

Contents

Series Editors' Foreword

It was in 1985 that large groups of Tamils who had fled following the pogrom of 1983 in Sri Lanka, the immediate antecedent of the war that had just begun in earnest on the island, arrived in Britain. Their stigmatisation as 'illegal arrivals' was an early episode in the escalating campaign against asylum seekers and refugees in many parts of the world in the decades to come. As far as Tamil asylum seekers are concerned, this campaign has been particularly virulent in Australia since the late 1990s.

▶ *Survival Media* is 'located in the space-time of the aftermath' of the war in Lanka and is written from within the experience of the Tamil diaspora. Although the war did not strike the author 'with the same direct and ferocious violence that so many others have experienced', Suvendrini Perera calls it 'the determining factor' of her life. This gives an idea of the intensity of her engagement and writing. Words of poets, sounds, images draw lines of flight, which end up bringing the reader back to the scene—to the 'fatal shores'—of the war.

The colonial past of Lanka, as the author effectively shows in the introduction, intertwines in Lanka with a postcolonial landscape crisscrossed by 'lethal checkpoints of Sinhala nationalism', by the rise of a twin Tamil nationalism, by failed development and modernisation projects, which further nurtured the nativist imaginary and 'a favourite myth of Sinhala ethnonationalism: that of a Buddhist age of plenty before the arrival of Tamils on the scene'. A 'relentless ethnicization of everyday life at the levels of the social landscape' sets the stage for the war,

DOI: 10.1057/9781137444646.0002

with anti-Tamil pogroms in 1958 and 1983 being matched by the rise of a Tamil nationalism that, in the 'exclusionary imaginary of separatism practiced by the LTTE', ended up refracting 'the Sinhala supremacism it took up arms against'. The massacre of Mullivaikkal in the last days of the war, the genocidal violence of the Lankan army, the 'callous indifference' demonstrated by the LTTE towards Tamil civilians, suicide bombings, and mass rapes build the 'horrorist' and 'necropolitical' thread that runs through the pages of *Survival Media*.

'This is not a story to pass on', Toni Morrison writes in her novel, *Beloved*.[1] Seaming together 'then' and 'now', working the boundaries between 'there' and 'here', the distances and proximities, Perera stages in this book an intense dialogue with 'diasporic Tamils' who, like herself, have tried to cope with the trauma of the war. The logics of translation and entanglement that make up the diasporic, according to Stuart Hall,[2] shape the writing and the language of the following pages. The rhythms of hip-hop and rap in M.I.A.'s music, the images of films and the words of Tamil diasporic writers compose a chorus that iterates the experience of the war, while at the same time, in a syncopated and abrupt way, opening up spaces of precarious hope.

This is a book about the war in Lanka and the cultural politics of diasporic Tamils. But war and diaspora are here also mirrors in which the experiences of dispossession and abjection of asylum seekers, refugees, and migrants are powerfully reflected. Perera describes the hardening of citizenship law in the UK and Australia, the persistence of colonial violence that targets non-white subjects in the global cities, and the 'theaters of cruelty'[3] that are migrant detention centers, through embodied instances which resonate in multiple ways with the scenes of war in Lanka.

And yet the politics of migration that is at stake in this book is not only a politics of dispossession and abjection. At the borders of the political, in the 'enactments of citizenship' performed by migrants and asylum seekers, new political habitations of the world emerge; the nation's 'impossible subjects' as Mae Ngai refers to them, persist in inscribing their mundane and stubborn lines of flight from the cage and misery of what is currently politically possible. 'It is on lines of flight that new weapons are invented, to be turned against the heavy arms of the State', write Gilles Deleuze and Felix Guattari in *A Thousand Plateaus*.[4] The survival media analysed here are such weapons: weapons of the weak, part and parcel of what Chela Sandoval terms the 'methodology of the

DOI: 10.1057/9781137444646.0002

oppressed' that is 'formulated and taught out of the shock of displacement, trauma, violence and resistance'.[5]

Survival Media contributes to our Mobility & Politics series by opening new angles on diaspora studies, as well as on the politics of borders and mobility. It is compelling reading, which navigates through memories and images of war, movements and practices of flight from desperate situations, and 'the soaring hopes and aspirations of those in flight'. Is this not the stuff many experiences of mobility are made from in the contemporary world?

Sandro Mezzadra, University of Bologna,
Member of the Mobility & Politics Global Advisory Board

The Series Editors:
Martin Geiger, Carleton University
Parvati Raghuram, Open University
William Walters, Carleton University

Notes

1   Toni Morrison (1987) *Beloved: A Novel* (New York: Plume), 274, 275.
2   Stuart Hall (2012) 'Avtar Brah's Cartographies: Moment, Method, Meaning', *Feminist Review* 100: 27–38.
3   Joseph Pugliese (2001) 'Penal Asylum: Refugees, Ethics, Hospitality', *Borderlands* 1(1), http://www. borderlands.net.au/vol1no1_2002/pugliese.html.
4   Gilles Deleuze and Félix Guattari (1987) *A Thousand Plateaus: Capitalism and Schizophrenia*, trans. Brian Massumi (London: Athlone Press), 226.
5   Chela Sandoval (2000), *Methodology of the Oppressed* (Minneapolis: Minnesota University Press), 77–8.

DOI: 10.1057/9781137444646.0002

In Lieu of...

Already I begin with a stutter, unable to find a proper name adequate to the geography I wish to invoke. *Sri* (auspicious, blessed, holy) *Lanka* invokes a natural unity, an island-nation, in this instance one that also claims divine authorisation through its adoption of the Sinhala character, *Sri*, in its title. The introduction of this character on the licence plates of cars and buses sparked waves of protest in the Tamil areas of the country in the 1950s, almost 20 years before *Sri Lanka* replaced the colonial name *Ceylon* in 1972. But this already gets me too far into the story. *Ceylon, Lanka, Eelam* (and a whole prior genealogy of names: *Taprobane, Serendib, where man alone is vile,* etc.) are all too partial, too fraught, too freighted with bad history. As a poor compromise, I hit on *Lanka, Illangai* in Tamil, as distinguished from the separatist homeland, *Eelam,* sought by the Liberation Tigers of Tamil Eelam (LTTE). *Sri,* both as a compressed ideology and an aspiration or injunction, a little like the 'Great' in Great Britain, is mostly dispensed with in the rest of this book, except when citing official documents.

Equally difficult to designate are the subjects of this most banal of academic conventions, the list of acknowledgements. Many colleagues, friends and family, from Lanka, Australia and elsewhere, diasporic and otherwise, have contributed to the making of this book. I have chosen, after much hesitation and indecision, to name none of them here. Taking inspiration from T. Shanaathanan's *The Incomplete Thombu,* I offer instead a personal and partial inventory of places and objects lost and found in the writing of this book. *The Incomplete Thombu,* a register or

DOI: 10.1057/9781137444646.0003

inventory, is a collection of hand-drawings by Jaffna residents displaced between 1983 and 2009, the duration of the long war. The pencilled sketches trace floor plans of houses lost and left, spare maps that situate homes that no longer exist in relation to adjacent buildings and to trees or rivers, the essential landmarks of a reconstituted landscape of loss and desire.

In lieu of names, then, an affective and intellectual cartography: the causeway at Elephant Pass shimmering in the sunshine; the winding ascent home to Hatton from Colombo via the Ginigaththena Road; my grandmother's house in Chundukulli, and a circle of half-remembered family compounds in Eechchamattai, Kopai and Chavakacheri; Chithankerni, from where they fetched fresh water for me when I would not drink from the salty well; a red and white garden; the Peretha Canteen at Vidyalankara; Wellawatte beach, whose sunsets I sometimes recall from my desk in Fremantle, Western Australia. Other places, artefacts and metonyms, too, enter this wandering narrative: the orange-brick haven of Melbourne in 1983; a black swan cresting the leaden waters; great wrought-iron gates off Amsterdam Avenue; the rooftops of occupied East Jerusalem; a buried history in lemon trees; boats aflame in mid-ocean. Always, the smoke of burning bridges.

*   *   *

Grateful acknowledgements for permission to quote from their works to Jean Arasanayagam, V.V. Ganeshananthan, M. Kannan, the French Institute of Pondicherry and Penguin India; special thanks to the family of the late Rajani Thiranagama for allowing me to quote from one of her poems. A number of sections in the book have been published previously and are presented here in extracted or revised form: 'In Flight: Castaways and the Poetics of Survival', *Griffith Review* 47 (2015); 'Missing in Action: By All Media Necessary', *Borderlands e-journal* 11.1 (2012); 'White Shores of Longing', *Continuum: Journal of Media & Cultural Studies*, 23.4 (2009); 'The Landscapes of Massacre' in *Torture and the Human Body*, ed. Shampa Biswas and Zahi Zalloua (Seattle: University of Washington Press, 2011). A version of Chapter 4 was presented as a keynote address at the Postcolonial Justice conference in Berlin in 2014, and published in different form in *Borderlands e-journal* 14.1 (2015). Some of the research for this book was made possible by grants from the Asia-Australia-Pacific Institute at Curtin University and the Australian Research Council.

Finally, my sincerely thanks to the series editors for the invitation to contribute to the Mobility & Politics series.

DOI: 10.1057/9781137444646.0003

Preface: The Location of the Aftermath

Shortly after the savage end to the savage 30-year war in Sri Lanka in May 2009, a video filmed on a phone camera made global headlines. It showed the naked, blindfolded body of a man, hands bound, legs spread-eagled, being forced down into marshy ground. It is a healthy, whole, body, muscled and well-fleshed, nothing like the wasted civilians who emerged from the war zone in their scraggly, broken groups, night after night on our TV screens in the global north. This one is fighting fit: a soldier, most likely a member of the defeated Liberation Tigers of Tamil Eelam (LTTE). There is a palpable squelch as the splayed body is violently pushed down into the mud. Seconds later, the man shudders, and we sense, rather than hear, the convulsive impact of bullet on flesh. This reflex of an imploding body, experts will later testify, is impossible to fake.

Another blindfolded and bound body buckles and falls on the marshy ground, next to the first. An unseen voice jeers, *How they jump*: this is easy work. The hand that holds the phone camera swivels slowly to show several more bodies, all naked, solid, prone on the ground, anomalously brown against the fresh green of the grass, the silver shimmer of water.

The video is replayed many times over ensuing months on the BBC, CNN and on various Internet sites, while the Lankan government persistently denies its veracity. Finally, the UN Special Investigator on Extrajudicial, Summary and Arbitrary Executions declares that a succession of experts in forensics, photography and the movement of the human body have all determined that it cannot be other than authentic (UN 2010).

Whenever I see this execution video (often in the months after it was first released), I think of fragments from a poem copied on the door of a women's toilet at the university where I work in Western Australia: *Between the coconut palms the graves are full/of ruined bones, of speechless death-rattles . . . the dead voices . . . the blue mouths freshly buried.*

What was going through her mind, the woman who carefully wrote down in English the 20 or so lines of a Spanish poem, standing in the unquiet anonymity of a toilet stall? What welling up of emotions, what compulsion of pain or outflow of rage, compelled her to copy out, or perhaps rewrite from memory, in deliberate black texta, these precise and terrible lines?

There are days when I scrutinise the faces of the students and co-workers who go in and out of our building. We are from many places here, other places of war and death, a community of elsewheres that we acknowledge only furtively in quick second glances and half-smiles. Pablo Neruda wrote *Los Dictadores*, published as part of his Latin American epic, *Canto General*, in the 1930s and 1940s. It was published in Mexico in 1950. Anyone could have copied out these lines of English translation, or transcribed them from memory on a toilet door some time in 2008 or 2009. Is it the one place she feels free from observation, a survivor of some murderous quagmire? Or is it someone who coldly wills herself there, in a field of mud and coconut palms? Did her nostrils swell as she wrote, filling unbearably with that mix of *blood and body, a penetrating/petal that brings nausea?*

There are many places, too many to enumerate, poisoned by the penetrating petal that betrays the pervasive, unspoken presence of hidden graves. But Lankans make special claims on Neruda, who was Chile's Consul in Ceylon from 1927 to 1929. He would describe Ceylon later as the place where he spent his bitterest hours and wrote many of his best poems. It is an intimate landscape that those lines call up, one unseen, unspoken, yet too well known:

> The weeping cannot be seen, like a plant
> whose seeds fall endlessly on the earth,
> whose large blind leaves grow even without light.
> Hatred has grown scale on scale,

DOI: 10.1057/9781137444646.0004

blow on blow, in the ghastly water of the swamp,
with a snout full of ooze and silence.

Pablo Neruda, Los Dictadores[1]

This book is located in the space-time of the aftermath. As described further in Chapter 1, the term 'survival media' is one I adopt to encompass the expressive forms through which Tamil migrant, refugee and diasporic subjects engage with the war in Lanka from the location of the aftermath. For many such, perhaps like the woman I picture above, the war is often an event known both intimately and at a remove, geographically and temporally distanced and textually mediated. Their preoccupations, hesitations, questions and hauntings cannot but diverge from those of subjects engaging with the imperatives and complexities of a troubled present and future in the former war zone and within Lanka.

The invitation by the editors to contribute to the Mobility & Politics series was an opportunity to bring together a number of questions that have preoccupied me over the years: on discourses and technologies of state terror, on geographies of violence and the policing of borders, on the cultural politics of asylum seeking and diaspora, on the limits of international justice. A frayed and sometimes imperceptible thread running through this body of work has been the 30-year war in Lanka. Yet I do not claim, in the terms of Qadri Ismail's evocative formulation, to have 'abided by Sri Lanka' over those long decades (Ismail 2005). The chapters that follow are perhaps more properly marked 'of no fixed abode'. Crisscrossing geographical, theoretical and disciplinary locations, they are offered here as a set of always partial and provisional reflections, intensities and hauntings from a state of absent presence and present absence, of being 'missing in action' (see Chapter 2).

At the same time, this book is grounded in the politics that surround the continuing presence of asylum seekers and refugees from the war in the global north. In these destinations, a clear understanding of the war and its aftermath is obscured both by the punitive approach of receiving states towards refugees and by the shallow rhetoric adopted by many opponents of state policies. As the triumphalist impunity assumed by the Lankan state finds ready partners in governments, such as that of Australia, desperate to 'stop the boats' and prevent the arrival of asylum seekers at any cost, opponents of these repressive migration policies all too often uncritically ally themselves with the destructive politics of remnants of the LTTE. In adopting a rhetoric that, as Rajan Hoole pithily

DOI: 10.1057/9781137444646.0004

puts it, capitalises on the 'afterglow of the LTTE', progressive and radical movements remain resolutely oblivious to long-standing and sustained critiques of secessionist nationalism from Tamil voices, both in Lanka and outside (2015, 142). Through these adoptions of LTTE narratives, refugees themselves are typecast or silenced, their complex histories overwritten.

In her carefully layered and detailed mapping of violence against women in the war, Sumathy calls for a shift in emphasis from 'rhetoric with its eyes turned on international agencies to a narrative form where the emphasis is on the "within"', insisting that 'the specificity of the struggle is waged at the nation, not outside its bounds' (forthcoming). This is a necessary caution directed at unrepresentative diasporics who wield political influence in the global north. Yet, despite the dangers posed by such unrepresentative interventions, the bounds of the nation are precisely what have been and continue to be at stake in the war, and 'the nation' cannot be a self-evident and taken for granted entity in the aftermath. Refugee, diasporic and migrant subjects from a range of political positions—the line between the 'voluntary' and 'involuntary' departures and even between 'refugee' and 'economic migrant' are not always easily drawn—remain keenly involved in and are mobilised by the struggles 'at the nation'. The ethico-political force of their engagement is not easily dismissed. Rather than an attempt to distinguish between subjects from the standpoint of a geographically bounded national space, I propose a heterogeneity of diasporic voices as subjects implicated, from differential and always partial locations, 'at the nation'. This book refutes the notion of a singular 'Tamil diaspora' as deployed by both the Lankan state and 'the international community'.

Questions of past and present can no more to be taken as given than those of location, of inside and outside, in the chapters that follow. Five years after its conclusion, the war continues to unfold across borders and in time: in the troubled passages of refugees and those asylum seekers held in the limbo of immigration camps in the global north or in secret security detention and other forms of statelessness; in the (albeit partial and compromised) form of transnational investigations and inquiries; in the unfinished stories of the disappeared and the unmarked graves of the lost. Even as weeds and victory monuments sprout on former battlegrounds, the location of the aftermath signals that here there is no clear sense of an ending. The aftermath is the site of an inability to draw a line, where the space of survival for the future cannot be disentangled

DOI: 10.1057/9781137444646.0004

from an ethical responsibility to that which cannot be simply someone else's past.

Note

1 The translation I am citing here appears on a number of websites, but I have not been able to find its published source. See http://famouspoetsandpoems.com/poets/pablo_neruda/poems/15737.

DOI: 10.1057/9781137444646.0004

List of Abbreviations

COIN	counterinsurgency
CSZ	Civilian Security Zone
HRW	Human Rights Watch
ICEP	International Crimes Evidence Project
ICG	International Crisis Group
LLRC	Lessons Learnt and Reconciliation Commission
LTTE	Liberation Tigers of Tamil Eelam
NFZ	No Fire Zone
OHCHR	Office of the High Commissioner for Human Rights
ULF	United Left Front
UNCT	United Nations Country Team
UNHCHR	United Nations High Commissioner for Human Rights
UNHRC	United Nations Human Rights Council
UNITAR/UNOSAT	United Nations Institute for Training and Research—Operational Satellite Applications Programme
UNRC	United Nations Resident Coordinator
UTHR [J]	University Teachers for Human Rights (Jaffna)

DOI: 10.1057/9781137444646.0005

Introduction—Lethal Imaginaries of Nationalism: A Brief History in Checkpoints

Abstract: *This is a brief introduction to ethnic biopolitics in Sri Lanka from the immediate postindependence period to the end of the war. It tracks the ethnicization of everyday life, social space and the body and suggests that ideologies of Sinhala supremacism underpinned both the socialist and neoliberal policies adopted by successive postindependence governments. It discusses the reactive nature of the Tamil separatist nationalism that emerged as the counterpart to Sinhala majoritarianism in its the various phases and the formations of Tamil diaspora nationalisms.*

Keywords: ethnic biopolitics; Black July; 'development' and retrogressive history in the postcolonial nation; diasporic subjects; enumerated communities in Lanka; Sinhala supremacism; Tamil diaspora

Perera, Suvendrini. *Survival Media: The Politics and Poetics of Mobility and the War in Sri Lanka.* New York: Palgrave Macmillan, 2016. DOI: 10.1057/9781137444646.0006.

President Mahinda Rajapaksa's victory speech the day after the conclusive defeat of the LTTE in May 2009 is as good a place as any to begin. Encouragingly, the president began his speech in Tamil. He declared: 'We should live in this country as children of one mother. No differences of race, caste and religion should prevail here' (2009). But what might appear to be an inclusive statement that places all citizens under the protective shade of a national umbrella registers, in the light of Lanka's recent histories, as a chilling erasure of difference. Indeed, Rajapaksa proceeded to declare that the word 'minorities' had been removed from the national lexicon more than three years earlier. Now there were just two kinds of people: those who loved the land of their birth and those who did not.

Rather than affirming the state as a multiethnic and multireligious polity, the speech denied legitimacy to the various linguistic, religious and ethnocultural groupings that constituted the population—not only the Tamils of the recently conquered north, but Muslims, Burgers and Malayaham Tamils, who were never part of the secessionist project. The body of the speech, delivered mostly in Sinhala, returned to the glories of the past and affirmed as national heroes the Sinhala kings of the Buddhist epic, the *Mahavamsa*, claimed as the authorising source for Sinhala ownership over the island in its entirety. The speech thus explicitly reaffirmed the nation in the image of the dominant and reasserted its territorial sovereignty over the island as a unified entity.

Although Rajapaksa's speech contained the strands of what could have been read as an inclusive narrative for the nation, the message of Sinhala ethnoreligious dominance was powerfully reinforced by the ways in which citizens were disciplined into participating in the state's victory in the days immediately after the LTTE's surrender. These jubilations, Valentine Daniels notes, had a grotesquely carnivalesque and hallucinogenic character (Bavinck 2011, 11–12). In Colombo, passers-by were hailed on the streets and offered a mouthful of *kiribath* (rice cooked in coconut milk) to celebrate the national victory. The seemingly inclusive gesture was again loaded. Tamils and Sinhalese both eat a form of this meal to mark auspicious occasions, such as the New Year, but they are very distinctive dishes—Sinhala kiribath is seasoned with salt and eaten with savoury accompaniments; its Tamil counterpart, *pukkai*, is sweetened, usually with dark brown palm sugar, and eaten with fruit. What was enacted in this seemingly inclusive move, then, was a powerful movement of coercive incorporation into an ethnicised body politic,

DOI: 10.1057/9781137444646.0006

and into what Roshan De Silva Wijeyeratne bluntly names 'the Sinhalese State' (2012, 403).

For many Tamils, this moment of hailing into the national carries frightening reminders of other checkpoints, at which those seen as extraneous to the nation faced shibboleths to test the limits of their belonging. In the pogroms of 1958 and 1983, citizens who could not or would not recite a stanza of Buddhist scripture, or pronounce certain everyday words the Sinhala way ('bucket', say, or 'window') were beaten or murdered. Ernest MacIntyre's play, *Rasanayagam's Last Riot*, is a reminder of this history. It ends with a scene of Rasanayagam being burned alive for uttering the Tamil word *baliya* (or *valiya*) instead of the Sinhala '*balthiya*' (MacIntyre 1990). Many lives turned on differences as slight as this small sibilance: the shape of an earring under a woman's hair, a speck of sandalwood or smear of ash on a forehead.

Only a small mouthful of festive kiribath, but it sticks in the gullet; in it are contained an entire spectrum of biopolitical practices and technologies that organised everyday life since the first decade of independence. That compulsory bite of kiribath is symbolic of a forced diet of national myths and fabricated histories, the production of enumerated identities, and the spatial technologies and geoimaginaries that recast the nation as a sacred Buddhist possession. Buttressing these mundane technologies are acts of discriminatory linguistic and religious legislation and continuing practices of extreme violence, including occupation, and the disappearing, torture and rape of dissidents through the operations of 'the shadow-state' (Thomson-Senanayke, 2014, 2).

This introductory chapter presents a partial and, at times, personal inventory of the lethal checkpoints of Sinhala extremist nationalism, and of its offshoot and counterpart, Tamil militarist nationalism, to ground the narratives that follow. The checkpoint as a constitutive feature of the social landscape is explored by Pradeep Jeganathan in terms of its 'anticipation of violence' for Tamil subjects in Colombo (2002, 360) and by Jennifer Hyndman and Malathi de Alwis in their discussion of the border zones of the north and east, where the state and the LTTE both imposed elaborate mechanisms to interrogate, track and harass selected groups within their territory (2005; Spencer et al., 2015). I deploy the term 'checkpoint' to signify both sites of symbolic violence where identities and allegiances are policed through shibboleths and other forms of coercive scrutiny and the material features of a landscape of state violence characterised by militarization, occupation and fear.

DOI: 10.1057/9781137444646.0006

The biopolitics of Sinhala supremacism

The intractable ethnoracial politics of present-day Lanka can be tracked to the disastrous conjoining of two broad systems of differentiation, indigenous and colonial, in the nineteenth and early twentieth centuries. In the decades leading up to independence from Britain in 1948, long-established but fluctuating local distinctions within a series of interconnected multiethnic and multireligious societies (marked by variations of language, religion, caste, and region) became inextricably entangled with, and were folded into, the grand categories of colonial racial classification. While twentieth-century European history provides one kind of evidence for the destructive coalescing of two different orders of racial signification in the term 'Aryan', the story of Lanka offers a less familiar instance of that same vicious entanglement. In a key essay, Kumari Jayawardena tracks how in Lanka, and elsewhere, the classifications of William Jones and other orientalists, based on the construct of an 'Indo-Aryan' group of languages, were disastrously transposed into a raciological register (Jayawardena 1983). From the late nineteenth century, the loose identifications of Sinhala and Tamil, and vague references to historical invaders in texts such as the Buddhist epic, *Mahavamsa*, were reordered to correspond with the loaded racialised categories of Aryan and Dravidian, setting in train a long, painful history of ethnoracial consolidation.

These divides were in turn cemented by the workings of colonial forms of ethnic/racial accounting and biopolitics. What Arjun Appadurai names 'enumerated communities' (1993) were brought into being in those colonies where race/ethnicity became the chosen principle of imperial governance. Appadurai details the processes that produced enumerated communities through the colonial census, conjoining 'the utilitarian needs of fiscal militarism in the world system, the classificatory logics of orientalist ethnography, the shadow presence of western democratic ideas of numerical representation, and the general shift from a classificatory to a numerical bio-politics' (1993, 333). The colonial census and its apparatus of calculation, aggregation and categorisation contributed to the making of 'self-consciously enumerated communities...embedded in...wider official discourses of space, time, resources, and relations' (ibid.).

Multiple and shifting prior gradations of difference in language, class, caste, religion and region solidified into racial and ethnic attributes

DOI: 10.1057/9781137444646.0006

through an essentialising calculus that would produce 'them' and 'us' in a communally or ethnoracially ordered society. In the post-independence era, enumeration and numerical representation were invariably linked to constructions of separate 'communal', 'racial' or 'ethnic' groups and became, critically, the chosen technologies through which decolonising states sought to redress colonial injustices and fashion the new nation (Krishna 1999). Post-independence politicians chose to heighten or build on differences among ethnic and religious groups in a confused amalgam of anti-western rhetoric, reinvention/reclaiming of colonised identities and the recourse to ethnic arithmetic.

Among the first of these major turning points was the enacting of what was popularly known as the 'Sinhala Only Act' in 1956. Under this legislation, which enshrined Sinhala as the official language, Tamils employed by the state were required to demonstrate written and spoken proficiency in Sinhala, regardless of whether or not this was relevant to their employment or the terms under which they had been hired (DeVotta 2004). The convoluted passage of the legislation in the year of the Buddha Jayanthi, the 2500th anniversary of the Buddha's death, was marked by competitive chauvinism by the major political parties and the escalation of ethnonationalist violence that would culminate in the anti-Tamil pogroms of 1958. My father was one of many thousands of Tamils to resign from government employment in protest at the Sinhala Only legislation. Shortly afterwards, a 'tar brush campaign' was initiated against signs bearing Tamil lettering, extending even to our quiet hill town. My earliest impressions date from this period: being carried across a railway line at night to avoid an approaching mob; the sight of my father's brass doctor's sign with a thick smear of tar across its tri-lingual lettering. The Sinhala-Only legislation and its aftermath was also a galvanising event for Tamil nationalism, which had developed in tandem with Sinhala nationalism since the latter half of the nineteenth century.

Another pivotal period was the landslide electoral victory in 1970 of a coalition of centre left, socialist and communist parties, known as the United Left Front (ULF). The ULF's unprecedented electoral majority provided the mandate for sweeping changes to the constitutional structure that had been in place since independence in 1948. The changes included changing the country's name from 'Ceylon' to 'Sri Lanka' and declaring a republic. Most significantly, a new constitution was promulgated, granting Buddhism the 'foremost place' in the land and enjoining on the state the duty 'to protect and foster Buddhism' (Welikala 2012).

DOI: 10.1057/9781137444646.0006

Other religions were assured of certain stipulated rights, but were emphatically put in second place. The political consequences of these constitutional changes have been widely discussed (Welikala 2012). Less attention has been given to the cultural and social impact of the accompanying measures that were imposed by the ULF in an attempt to refashion the nation in spatial and temporal terms. These can be best understood as a concentrated effort to reorder the spaces and practices of everyday life in ways that combined anti-colonial and socialist rhetoric with ethnoreligious nationalism and biopolitical management. Along with the ULF's brutal suppression of the leftist uprising in the south in 1971, a prelude to the war in the north to come, the 1970s were characterised by the relentless ethnicisation of everyday life, including the built environment, the soundscape and the performative practices of the body. Dress, speech, diet and deportment were all disciplined and marked through ethnicised practices. The spatiotemporal recoding of everyday life in terms of an imagined Buddhist order extended to the calendar. In place of the biblical seven-day week, the machinery of the entire state was shifted to an arrangement based on the four phases of the moon that constitute the Buddhist almanac. As a schoolgirl during this period, I remember most clearly that school might run for four, five or six days, depending on the variable number of days in a given week. Public space on city streets and at junctions was claimed as Buddhist Sinhala space by the planting of *bodhi* (or 'bo') trees and the erection of temples on land where a sapling might be sighted. As the tree under which the Buddha is said to have reached enlightenment, these were accorded sacred status. Broadcasts via loudspeakers of Buddhist sermons and chants at prescribed times were another means by which neighbourhoods and public spaces in the vicinity of temples were claimed as Buddhist. The reorientation of the practices of everyday life at spatial, temporal and corporeal levels involved the mobilisation and regulation of ethnoreligious identities through a set of biopolitical processes. This included issuing identity cards that, for the first time, included information on ethnicity and place of birth.

The most explosive of the ULF's discriminatory acts was the introduction of university admission legislation intended to promote opportunities for Sinhala and Muslim students while curtailing those for students from the Tamil areas of the north. Again, this bore the progressive face of affirmative action for rural youth—the generation educated primarily in Sinhala as post-independence *swabasha* (indigenous language)

DOI: 10.1057/9781137444646.0006

policies came to fruition. Although its rhetorical-ideological mode was anti-western and socialist, the policy added to the sense of lives increasingly organised through the principles of ethnic arithmetic, and directly targeted at diminishing opportunities for Tamils, represented as having benefitted inordinately from colonial rule.

Another outbreak of anti-Tamil pogroms in 1976 fuelled the sense of a community increasingly under attack and led to a wave of Tamil departures abroad. This was the environment in which Tamil militant secessionist ideologies and counter-notions of an historically distinct Tamil identity began to gain a serious following, especially among young men and women in the north who had been deprived of university admission. What became known as the Vaddukoddai Resolution, passed by a group of Tamil parties in 1976, would be taken as a manifesto for separatism, although by some accounts, it was adopted as 'a negotiating position' only (Hoole 2015, 158–9).

The coexistence of exclusionary ethnonationalism and ardent anti-colonialism in the policies of the ULF government is rendered intelligible by Kamala Visweswaran's argument that, in the cases of India, Sri Lanka and elsewhere, 'the overthrow of European colonialism resulted in the next cycle of settler-colonialism, wherein one nation's anti-colonialism would become another (captive) nation's experience of colonialism' (2012, 442). Visweswaran contends that postcolonial theory has tended to elide the colonialist aspects of post-independence states, and thus misrecognised the liberationist politics of the armed secessionist movements that emerged in opposition to them. As I explore below, many aspects of Sinhala expansionism into the northeast in the 1960s and 1970s are indeed settler-colonialist in effect. However, to understand the Tamil regions of Lanka as a captive 'nation-within-a-nation' posits Tamil and Sinhala identities already constituted as separate and inimical entities, an understanding that overwrites long histories of overlap, intermingling, collaboration and coexistence (Silva 2002), as well as the marked fissures of ethnicity, religion and caste among Tamil-speaking groups and regions themselves. A more nuanced characterisation of ethnic relations in Lanka might be that the logic of 'two nations' was violently produced from within and without in the years following independence, not as an inevitable outcome, but as the effect of a set of contingent and variable factors, an outgrowth of choices and practices by the state—and by those who sought to resist its ethnonationalism.

DOI: 10.1057/9781137444646.0006

In the case of the emergence of the LTTE, the danger of Visweswaran's analysis is the elision of the extent to which militant opposition movements themselves reproduce the very ideologies they seek to challenge, and indeed, reenact settler-colonialist violence towards other ethnicities within their claimed boundaries. Despite the hopeful insertion of terms such as 'liberation' and 'socialist' in their names, as a number of critics have commented, Tamil separatist movements of the 1980s were motivated by a reactive nationalism that failed to develop any deeper critical political consciousness or theoretical analysis (Hoole 2015).

The sharpest and most astute criticisms of militant Tamil nationalism have emerged from scholars who were most directly exposed to its violence, both in the crucible of the north and, more broadly, within Tamil and Muslim communities (Hoole et al. 1990; Sivanandan, 1984; Manikkalingam 1995; Sumathy 2001 and 2004; Shobasakthi 2012; Satkunananthan 2012; Subramanian 2014; Hoole 2015). The exclusionary imaginary of Tamil separatism practiced by the LTTE refracts the Sinhala supremacism it took up arms against. Its brutal violence was directed not only against the Lankan state and Sinhala civilians, but also at the Tamil and Muslim populations in the areas that it claimed as its homeland: 'Tamil Eelam'.

One of the LTTE's most egregious acts of violence was the expulsion of the entire Muslim population from the Tamil capital of Jaffna in 1990. In an act reminiscent of other sweeping evictions in the annals of ethnic cleansing, Tamil-speaking Muslims who had been part of the Jaffna society for centuries were brutally ejected at a few hours' notice, loaded onto trucks with little more than the clothes on their backs, in order to fulfil the LTTE's monoethnic vision of an exclusive 'Tamil Eelam'. The relegation of the Muslim populations of the north and east to the status of secondary citizens was characteristic of the Eelamist imaginary from the outset, as underlined by its insistence on the name 'Tamil Eelam' (Coomaraswamy and Perera-Rajasingham 2009, 120). The sense of grief and horrified misgiving which the expulsion of the Muslims evoked in many Tamils finds expression in V.I.S Jayapalan's poem, 'Ettavathu Pey':

> here comes the eighth ghost
> before it rolls our heads
> before it fills our princes'
> coffins with earth
> before it erases our poems
> and writes lamentations in the wind...

DOI: 10.1057/9781137444646.0006

oh my neighbour, oh my neighbour,
come back and save us
with those prayer calls
six times a day.

(trans. Whittington in Kannan, Whittington, Buck and Babu, 2014, 103)

Mythifying the present

Although religion was the marker that distinguished the Tamil-speaking Muslims who were expelled from the Jaffna peninsula, the imaginary of Tamil separatism does not appear to be driven by the same totalising ethnoreligious ideology as that of Buddhist supremacism, but is rather based on a sense of linguistic and spatial identity constituted by the forces of Sinhala exclusionary nationalism, rather than pre-existing it. The spatiotemporal recasting of the nation during the 1970s to reflect Sinhala Buddhist supremacism and sense of ownership over its entirety was most forcefully demonstrated in the revival of an imagined past in the present. The *Mahavamsa,* a chronicle written in the ancient language of Pali, dating back to the sixth century BCE, is the authorising document of the Buddhist project in Lanka. Beginning with the myth of the dying Buddha's nomination of the island of Lanka as the chosen future domicile of Buddhism, it presents the ultimate source for both contemporary ethnoreligious exceptionalism (Lankan Buddhists as the faith's true custodians and chosen people) and the state's claim to indivisible sovereignty over the land, conceptualised in the form of a territorially complete entity, the island. Territorial sovereignty and Buddhist ethnoreligious supremacy thus became deeply enmeshed with, and continue to underwrite, the investment in the structure of the unitary state of Sri Lanka (see also Jazeel 2009).

Overlaying this mytho-religious authorisation is the spatial-geographical imaginary of Sri Lanka, literally, blessed or holy island. In my writings on Australia, I elaborate on the implications of the island as a geographical figure that represents for the colonising white imagination a singular, self-contained and unified entity: one that is insulated from the threatening geography of 'Asia', by which it is encircled (Perera 2009). For the Sinhala Buddhist imaginary, continually beset by fears of being overwhelmed by its giant neighbour, India, the self-enclosed and insulated form of the island holds a similar reassurance. The geographical

DOI: 10.1057/9781137444646.0006

form of the island, figured as Buddhism's preordained abode, is thus indissociable from the project of territorial sovereignty in contemporary Sinhala ethnonationalist politics, and explains the implacable opposition, not only to the prospect of Tamil separatism, but even to other forms of spatial reorganisation, such as federalism or regional devolution. The territorial imaginary of Sinhala Buddhist supremacism continues to underpin seemingly opposed political and economic programs, such as the socialist agenda of the 1970s and the neoliberalism that has increasingly dominated since the 1980s.

In the 1970s, the project of asserting sovereignty over and (re)claiming of the land as Buddhist territory became closely bound up with the trope of development, particularly in the border regions between the Jaffna peninsula and the Sinhala-dominated south. Again, the rhetorical and ideological space between 'progressive' and 'reactionary' discourses is deeply mystified by ethnoreligious ideologies. In the 1970s and 1980s, the north-central and eastern provinces of Lanka, the regions of the country that later would become the ground for some of the most intense battles of the war, were the target of numerous 'Development' and 'Green Revolution' programs that entailed no less than the imposition of a new ecology. Irrigation schemes were designed to divert rivers and build tanks and dams to support the production of cash crops for urban and export markets, replacing local cultivations of staple foods. Crucially, this would necessitate introducing new sources of labour, premised on 'internal colonisation' schemes from the south. This was coupled with the engineering of a shift in the ethnic mix of the population, from predominantly Tamil and Muslim or multiethnic communities, to settlers who were predominantly Sinhala.

The development and resettlement schemes of the 1970s were underpinned by a scholarship of conjectured heritage. Dubious etymologies provided the justification for changing ancient place names in an attempt to expunge the historical presence of the ethnic other from the imagined national heartland. Historical and archaeological studies channelled anti-colonial or anti-imperialist energies into a narrow and exclusionary Sinhala ethnonationalism that, paradoxically, was also informed by orientalist images and tropes. Development and modernity, then, were both harnessed to 'the mythohistoriography of the Sinhalese [that] has become indispensable to the political order' (Kleinfeld 2005, 289).

At another level, the potent appeal of a dream of progress yoked to a mythical past owed much to the transnational circulation of the Zionist

DOI: 10.1057/9781137444646.0006

model in the period following the Second World War. State-sponsored programs promised landless peasants and urban poor a new start in the border zones of the north-west and east, ostensibly to consolidate a genuinely national consciousness. As projects of 'internal colonisation', these schemes harnessed a sense of sacred mission to the new dawn of modernity, socialism and nation-building. In practice, as in the case of Palestine, these new settlements and development projects actively undermined multiethnic relations that already existed in these places. Valentine Daniel and Yuvaraj Thangaraj describe the effects in the areas around the eastern region of Batticaloa, where Buddhists and Hindus had once shared religious and cultural practices:

> Along with each settlement...came the building of a local Buddhist temple and the presence of a Buddhist priest. With the latter also came a form of Buddhism that was committed to purge folk elements of Buddhism from local Buddhist practices...The local Tamils who had hitherto partaken in what they...knew as common Buddhist-Hindu practices, were struck by the exclusivist self-definition of the new state Buddhism and reacted to it by withdrawing into an exclusive Hindu-Tamil definition of their own. The local Sinhalese, briefly caught in the middle, found the pressures of settler ridicule, on the one hand, and allures of state patronage, on the other, too much to resist, and their submission to and incorporation into a state-fabricated Sinhalese national culture was to be completed in short order. (Daniel and Thangaraj 1995, 222–3)

New settlers attempted to escape the dangerous environment that they had unwittingly entered, but were refused permission to depart. Instead, in the early years of the war they were appointed 'home guards' and provided with guns to serve as a buffer between the army and the guerrillas. So the scene was set for some of the war's most tangled and vicious clashes. Tortuous alliances and recombinations worked to reduce the complex multiethnicity of the region into the polarities of Sinhala versus Tamil and Tamil versus Muslim. A program ostensibly aimed at promoting national unification and producing an equitable society that redressed colonial injustices was experienced by all as an attempt to (re)establish Buddhist cultural and territorial dominance. Furthermore, it intensified ethnoreligious divides and hardened exclusionary identities in the decades that followed. Thirty years later, postwar discourses of unification are once again focused on discourses of Sinhala settlement in the war zone, the building of Buddhist temples and the establishment of military enterprises, indicating a continuation of, rather than a

DOI: 10.1057/9781137444646.0006

break with, these aspects of the Buddhist supremacist spatial imaginary (Haviland 2011, Spencer et al 2015).

Tamil diasporic lives and the aftermath

In 2010, a year after the war ended, an editorial in the Tamil newspaper, *Thinakkural*, published an editorial titled 'Show us a way to live' to mark the opening of the government's Lessons Learnt and Reconciliation Commission (LLRC), at Killinochchi, the administrative centre of the defeated LTTE. Between a plea and a command, the injunction 'Show us a way to live' conveys something of the profound dislocation experienced by those at the heart of a defeated territory. This is not to suggest that support for the LTTE was univocal, even on what they claimed as their home ground: as an increasing weight of evidence makes clear, under the LTTE, a gamut of terrorising measures was in place to crush internal dissent and exert a stranglehold on the population through practices such as conscription of children and summary execution (Bavinck 2011). The people of the north show scant desire for the return of LTTE rule (Mohan 2014, Subramanian 2014). Yet, regardless of whether they supported the LTTE, at the end of the war the people of Killinochchi and its surrounds, indeed of the entire north and east of Lanka, confronted a terrain of physical and psychic dislocation: blasted lands, dead and missing loved ones, lost homes and livelihoods, and the visible and invisible injuries of a 30-year conflict.

Against this backdrop, 'Show us a way to live' is a cry that resounds on a number of levels. At its most elemental, it refers to the immediate survival needs of local populations that remained unmet, especially for the most vulnerable. A 2011 report by the International Crisis Group (ICG) meticulously documented the conditions of poverty, homelessness and physical and economic insecurity among women, who continue to experience sexual violence and exploitation from both government forces who remain in the area to this day, and from local men. The whereabouts of family members who went missing, whether abducted or detained after their surrender, remain unknown, and new disappearances still occur. The north continues to be not only heavily militarised, but has seen the army move into the spaces of civilian life, through its operation of shops and businesses, cementing the sense of an occupation. Local residents often find that the homes and land they lost have been redistributed. There is ample evidence of government attempts to once

DOI: 10.1057/9781137444646.0006

again reengineer the population mix in the area and impose a Buddhist character on parts of the conquered territory. Ambitious development projects, housing for government and NGO workers, triumphal 'pilgrimages' to newfound Buddhist sites, domestic trophy tourism of war zones, and an influx of international visitors all seem to take precedence over housing those rendered homeless and destitute. The Muslim inhabitants of the north, who were forcibly evicted more than 20 years earlier by the LTTE's own attempt at ethnic cleansing, remain displaced, for the most part, in the south of the country.

This is a very incomplete catalogue of the appalling lack of basic conditions for living in the wake of the war. Yet, *Thinakkural's* exhortation also refers to something more. 'Show us a way to live' evokes not only the lack of the essential wherewithal, the means for living, but also, at the deepest level, the need for new directions in the beliefs, ideologies and affective investments that sustain and enable people and communities to continue living. This search for 'a way to live' involves a political, emotional and psychological reorientation and search for survival, not only for those in the immediate warzone, but also within diaspora groups who are perceived, or perceive themselves, as in some ways extensions of it, and whose everyday lives were, and are, materially and emotionally bound up with it.

Diasporic Tamils remain both subjects and objects, addressors and addressees, of the injunction, 'Show us a way to live'. Jacques Audiard's film, *Dheepan*, awarded the Palme d'Or at the Cannes film festival in 2015, follows the lives of Tamil refugees in France, tracing a continuity between the war zones in which the central characters move. In its 'allegorizing' of Paris as Colombo (Foundas 2015), and its blurring of the divide that marks conventional narratives of the global north as havens for refugees, Audiard suggests, once again, that 'there' and 'here' are not completely separable spaces. The film draws heavily on the autobiography of its star, Antonythasan Jesuthasan, a former child soldier of the LTTE and its fierce critic in his novels, written under the pseudonym Shobasakthi. Working at a series of menial jobs by day, and writing in Tamil in his spare time, Shobasakthi offers a moving account of the continuities between there and here, insisting that, despite his physical relocation in Paris, the life he was forced to leave behind remains his emotional, political and creative centre:

> To live in Sri Lanka and write is until this day, a life-threatening activity ... My living in Paris allows me to write freely. [But] ... those I wish to write about— their sorrows, the injustices that they have endured, their desires—I am

DOI: 10.1057/9781137444646.0006

forced to live ten thousand kilometers away from them in Paris, a factor that effectively blunts my writing. Rather than being in Paris, I wish I could live in Sri Lanka. Do wish me that I would be given that chance. (Shobasakthi 2012)

In search of 'the Tamil diaspora'

In the literature on diasporas shaped by war, diaspora Lankan Tamils are seen as distinctive in the level of influence they brought to bear on the conduct and duration of the war. Their financial and moral support was critical for the LTTE at certain stages of the war, as was the domestic political pressure they managed to exert in their new homes in North America and Europe. Less clearly understood, however, are the internal fractures and divisions that also characterised diaspora Tamils from the outset. Ahilan Kadirgamar is more nuanced than others in tracing the forces that established 'separatist Tamil nationalism as dominant within the diaspora' in the early 1990s, leading to 'the over-determination of separatist Tamil Eelam politics over other forms of collective politics both in relation to Lanka and in the context of refugee life in the west' (2010, 24). Less historicised analyses cast diasporic Tamils as a monolithic and unchanging entity, united by unconditional support for the LTTE throughout the 30-year period of the war. Even after the comprehensive defeat of the LTTE in 2009, this bogey of an intractable, war-mongering Tamil diaspora is invoked by Lankan government spokespeople and Sinhala ultra-nationalists as a means to keep anti-Tamil sentiments at fever pitch and to drum up hysteria against moves such as the calls for an international inquiry (see Chapter 4). At the same time, important Tamil voices caution that diasporic preoccupations, such as the pogroms of Black July and highly partisan accounts of the war's final days, should not obscure the different priorities of Tamil populations seeking a way to the future (Kadirgamar in Bastians 2015; Satkunananthan 2012).

Instead of the homogenising term, 'the Tamil diaspora,' I speak of diasporic Tamils, allowing for a more nuanced analysis of attitudes and positions about the war. The war, and in particular the 1983 pogrom that is generally agreed to have been the trigger point for it, was the impetus for the forced or voluntary departure of over a million Tamils from Lanka (I am one of them). Support among this group for the war waged by the LTTE, however, was by no means a given. The affective investments and emotional identifications in the project of separatist Tamil nationalism

DOI: 10.1057/9781137444646.0006

among diasporic subjects is in need of much more detailed analysis, not only among diasporic Tamils for whom the cause of Tamil Eelam or separatist nationalism constituted an ideological horizon, but also for those whose social worlds remain directly or indirectly entwined with it.

Diaspora cultural politics

Kadirgamar identifies pro-LTTE Tamil nationalist diasporic organisations as having three aspects: those 'of a liberation movement with exiled nationalist politics, a multinational corporation with attendant finances, operations and institutions, and a mafia with underworld and extortionist activities' (2010, 24). What is omitted here, or perhaps is reductively subsumed under the category of 'exiled nationalist politics', is the crucial dimension of cultural politics. These span a whole gamut of activities—from LTTE-sponsored events, such as 'Heroes' Day' and cultural festivals such as *Pongu Thamil*, to less structured spaces outside the LTTE's purview: cultural and religious gatherings, localised human rights and NGO activities, social occasions organised by community groups in Tamil or English, myriad popular cultural forms, and other spaces where stories of diasporic life and testimonies of war and displacement could be shared in safety. On the margins of separatist national politics, these spaces nonetheless may have overlapping memberships and interests, and have selectively deployed its rhetoric and symbols, both in order to engage with experiences of loss and trauma, and in more indirect ways, to forge communities of affiliation within the hostile or alien worlds in which Tamil migrants and refugees found themselves.

While direct opposition to the LTTE is less visible, except in writers such as Shobasakthi, some of these contradictions and complexities of diasporic Tamil lives are captured in the work of new diasporic generations. Their affective investments and identifications range from the Tamil-Canadians or -Australians who are unshakable in their allegiance to the Eelamist cause, to those whose cultural and emotional landscapes have been shaped at a more or less unconscious level by the politics of the post-1983, pro-LTTE diaspora. At another level are those whose everyday lives are deeply entwined culturally and socially, although not necessarily politically and ideologically, with the pro-LTTE diaspora. *Love Marriage*, a 2008 novel by V.V. Ganeshananthan, a member of the younger generation of North American diaspora Tamil authors, represents some of

DOI: 10.1057/9781137444646.0006

these contradictions. Its central character is a young woman called on to nurse her dying uncle, a former LTTE leader. Her response is ambivalent: revulsion at the violence and intolerance he represents, intermixed with a kind of admiration for the glamorized, heroic exploits of his youth. Was Ganeshananthan prescient in imagining the LTTE as aging and mortally ill? Or does the growing attraction and understanding the niece begins to feel for the dying man foreshadow a new generation of LTTE supporters in the diaspora?

Such questions point to the ways in which seeking or showing a 'way to live' play out within disparate diasporic communities, for those lives for whom the war in Lanka provided both the rationale and habitus, as well as for those more removed from it. If the notion of Eelam represented a kind of fatal, yet compelling, telos, which gathered into it various diasporic energies, desires, dreams and aspirations, either as a symbolic or actual place of return, how will these energies, dreams and desires be redirected in the future? How does the loss of the imagined homeland impinge on imagined futures and hopes in their new homes, both for those who subscribed to the goal of Eelam and those who didn't?

Scattered answerabilities

With the exception of *Palmyrah Fallen*, Rajan Hoole's rigorous calling to account of all parties, the handful of books in English to appear since the war are mostly works of reportage. The earliest, *The Cage,* is an account by UN official Gordon Weiss, who was located in Lanka in the weeks leading up to the international withdrawal from the war zone. Three books by foreign journalists followed: by BBC correspondent Frances Harrison, and two by Indian journalists, Rohini Mohan and Samanth Subramanian. In *The Divided Island*, Subramanian, a journalist from South India, travels fitfully across the country, his bouts of illness and recurring doubts about his project mirroring the febrile and uncertain state of the people he meets. The subjects he interviews move continually between the traumatic phases of the war that are still intensely present in their lives, such as the pogroms of 1983 and the killing fields of 2009, and the postwar everyday:

> Gradually, in my head, the boundaries between these slices of time—between wartime and post-war Sri Lanka—melted away. The phrase 'post war' had lost its meaning…Outright battle had stopped, but an unbroken arc of violence

DOI: 10.1057/9781137444646.0006

stretched from the war right into our midst…People still lived in fear, and some of them still died in sudden, unnatural ways. Anger still rippled through the island. (2014, 286)

The suspended state Subramanian refers to is one in which the war is officially over, yet anger and an 'unbroken arc of violence' still grip the land. Time shifts unpredictably backwards and forwards.

A similar heterochronicity, a simultaneity of 'slices of time', also characterises the interconnected chapters that follow. The first three chapters of the book focus on the embodied and expressive movements of refugee and diasporic groups during and after the war. Chapter 1 develops the concept of survival media in the context of people on the move, their covert and indirect trajectories over land and sea. Chapter 2 turns to the cultural and biographical productions of Maya Arulpragasam, the performer known as M.I.A., described as 'the most famous member of the Tamil diaspora' (Mackey 2009). Chapter 3 shifts between scenes of real and imagined arrival in Australia and London to track dramas of citizenship for what Mae Ngai terms the impossible subjects of nation, refugee and migrant arrivals in the states of the global North. At the centre of the chapter is a play, *Theatre of Migration*, directed by the influential Tamil-Australian dramatist Ernest Thalayasingham MacIntyre.

The last two chapters circle back to the bloody events of May 2009. Chapter 4 examines questions of accountability for the lives lost in its final days in terms of the claims and counterclaims of international justice. Its analysis centres on the satellite images recorded by various international agencies as forms of remote monitorship that represent, both metaphorically and materially, the hovering, telescopic oversight of international justice over this seemingly obscure war. Chapter 5 returns to the final battleground at Mullivaikkal and the acts of mass rape-torture that followed the LTTE's defeat. It attempts to situate the multivalent figure of the LTTE female cadre, most often imagined as a suicide bomber, within discursive economies of gender, nationalism and terror, as it also acknowledges the impossibility of a theoretical framework adequate to the violence that it inventories.

The presences and absences in the book, the traces and spectres that inhabit it, as I have already said, must differ from those of the local or the citizen. In his celebrated essay on Avtar Brah, Stuart Hall comes closest to outlining the practice of what he calls 'diasporic reasoning', and to naming the diasporic as itself an interpretive frame. The diasporic emerges at a political, historical and theoretical conjuncture as 'a specific

DOI: 10.1057/9781137444646.0006

structure of transformations, displacements and condensations'. Hall describes the diasporic as operating thorough a doubled inscription: like 'the figure in the carpet', it invokes the indeterminable and endlessly deferred labour of interpretation in Henry James' novella of that name, while simultaneously referencing a specific historical and social: 'the moment of the problematic of the subject—when critical thought comes face to face with the perplexing interface between the social and the psychic, the objective and the subjective in the historic'. The effects of diasporic double inscription are uncertain, spectral, incomplete; its logics of 'translation' and 'entanglement' are constituted by a language that continually 'breaks on you' (Hall 2012, 100).

Hall's formulations of the diasporic articulate best the theoretical, political and personal engagements that shape this project. In its breakages and lapses, ellipses and circularities are encoded the distances as well as the intimacies that constitute the relations of the there and here, the then and now; the scattered answerabilities to the war of subjects geographically unmoored by it, to resurface, and be refashioned, for better and worse, as migrants, refugees, diasporics.

DOI: 10.1057/9781137444646.0006

1
Lines of Flight: Survival Media

Abstract: *Chapter 1 develops the concept of survival media in the context of people on the move. Survival media encompass the embodied and expressive movements of survivors and refugees of the war and the practices and narratives, artefacts and apparatuses that constitute their flights, forced and free. Survival media include the spaces and geographies produced by refugee bodies moving over land and sea, the cultural forms they mobilise (testimonies, slogans and protests, media statements, hip-hop, poems, stories, and performances), as well as the affiliations and interconnections they engender and the new subjectivities and citizenships, social ecologies and transnational politics and poetics they bring into play.*

Keywords: Jaya Lestari; poetics of survival; refugee poetics; Yaguine Koïta and Fodé Tounkara

Perera, Suvendrini. *Survival Media: The Politics and Poetics of Mobility and the War in Sri Lanka.* New York: Palgrave Macmillan, 2016. DOI: 10.1057/9781137444646.0007.

On 9 April 2013, a boat carrying 67 asylum seekers from Lanka made its way undetected through several levels of security, to sail straight into the remote port of Geraldton, in Western Australia. It was lunch time, and diners at the local beachfront café could hardly believe their eyes: this overburdened and ramshackle craft was nothing like the agricultural and cargo ships that criss-cross this regional harbour. It would turn out that the boat had sailed all the way from the west coast of Lanka, across the Indian Ocean, to thread its way southwards through the Indonesian archipelago, undetected by elaborate surveillance and border security systems, into waters heavily patrolled by the Australian navy (Orr 2013). Customs officials and police were alerted to the presence of 'unauthorised maritime arrivals' off the beach, and lost little time cordoning off the scene and impounding the boat. But for a short while, the arrivals remained on board their incongruous craft and could be viewed and photographed for the local news.

Caught in the brilliant afternoon sunshine, silhouetted against a giant 'Welcome to Geraldton' sign, the castaway boat has an almost festive look. A jaunty blue trim offsets the cracks and rust stains on its hull. There is a stir and energy to the figures moving on deck. Curious children peer through the railings. A woman unfurls a thick plait of hair. You can just read the name on the prow, *Bremen,* and a corporate logo that identifies it as a gift of the tsunami aid effort, almost ten years ago. A makeshift banner atop the cabin declares the desired destination, New Zealand, and even bears a makeshift image of that country's flag. The boat, it seems, was making for friendlier shores than Australia before engine trouble forced the passengers to try their luck here, after 44 days at sea. A breeze lifts the homemade flag. A statement of intent and a call-out to the future, it flutters, then flies, for now, in the uncertain shelter of this strange harbour.

In flight: a double-edged phrase, whose Janus-face looks back and forward, betokening both the fears it seeks to escape, the terrors of the past and present, and the dare of joys ahead. Within fraught refugee geographies of peril and possibility, a voyage across oceans in a small boat, *flight* signifies at once the covert or embattled movements that attempt escape from desperate situations and the soaring hopes and aspirations of those in flight. Embodied movements of flight and escape are animated by flights of imagination and desire; they are the expressive media of high-flying hopes and dreams. *Flight* and *fancy:* here they allude to a poetics of survival that attends movements of terrified

DOI: 10.1057/9781137444646.0007

escape and the large and small acts of imagining that enable and sustain them—messages set afloat in plastic bottles, or held up high across razor wire, the name of a destination blazoned on a ship's mast, a letter stored on a washed up or frozen body—through the spaces of terror and blockage in which they are repeatedly ensnared. The sections of this chapter weave and veer across disjunctive, irreconcilable geographies of flight and fancy, the slices of time that entwine past and present, and the heterogeneous assemblages of human and non-human bodies, artefacts, elements, technologies and interrelations that encompass survival media for subjects in flight.

In his translation of Gilles Deleuze and Felix Guattari's *A Thousand Plateaus*, Brian Massumi glosses the term 'lines of flight' as 'not only the act of fleeing or eluding but also flowing, leaking, and disappearing into the distance (the vanishing point in a painting)'—though he specifies, 'It has no relation to flying' (Deleuze and Guattari 1980, xvi). My usage here encompasses the contingent and ephemeral trajectories of subjects on the run, the acts of disappearing, and the violent dispersals that attend them, as it also references the transformative and creative promise, at least, of Deleuzian lines of flight. In this chapter, and those that follow, survival media signify the embodied and expressive movements of survivors and refugees of the war, and the practices and narratives, artefacts and apparatuses that constitute their flights, forced and free. Survival media include the spaces and geographies produced by refugee bodies moving over land and sea, the cultural forms they mobilise (testimonies, slogans and protests, media statements, hip-hop, poems, stories, performances), as well as the affiliations and interconnections they engender, and the new subjectivities and citizenships, the social ecologies and transnational politics and poetics they bring into play.

Of flight—and fancy

The possibility and peril with which flight is fraught are perhaps most clearly embodied in the story of two 14-year-old boys from Guinea who stowed themselves away in the wheel-bay of a plane bound for Belgium. Found on their frozen bodies on landing was a letter, with the simple instruction, 'In case we die, deliver to Messrs. the members and officials of Europe' (Sullivan and Casert 2000). It was signed with their full names, Yaguine Koïta and Fodé Tounkara. In what they intended as

DOI: 10.1057/9781137444646.0007

their last testament, the boys assume the authority to speak, not only for themselves, but also for the youth of their entire continent:

> We have the honor and pleasure and great confidence in you to write this letter to talk to you of the objective of our journey and the suffering of us, the children and young people of Africa. . . . But first of all, we present to you our sweetest, most adoring and respectful salutations . . . You are for us, in Africa, the ones whom we must ask for help. We appeal to you, for the love of your continent, for the feelings you have toward your people and above all for the affinity and love you have for your children . . . Moreover, for the love and meekness of our creator, almighty God, who has given you all the good experience, wealth and power to build and organize well your continent to become the most beautiful and admirable of all. (ibid.)

The boys' language may be fanciful in more ways than one, yet it could not offer a more acute analysis of the forces that impel them into flight. Speaking as ambassadors for the children of Africa, they show a clear-eyed understanding of Europe's place as the continent that has built and organised itself so as to become the beneficiary of all 'good experience, wealth and power'. Of necessity, Europe becomes the prime source of support and aid, the power from whom, above all, the citizens of lesser continents *must* ask for help—even at the cost of their lives. A visa application from the grave, the letter articulates the compelling historical and geopolitical logic that set Yaguine and Fodé in motion, mobilising their bodies into flight from their small village in Guinea into the freezing metallic cavities of a plane bound for the Europe they will never reach.

Like countless others in flight by air, land and water, Yaguine Koïta and Fodé Tounkara represent the surplus of a geopolitical and economic order in which both their lives and deaths are rendered expendable, disposable, and finally, invisible. In Jenna Brager's acute analysis in the wake of the drowning of thousands of African migrants in the Mediterranean, this is an order that operates through a 'necropolitical creation of disposable classes that are prone to vanishing' (2015). This vanishing, however,' is not episodic or mysterious,' but 'traceable', linked in a 'genealogy of violence' to those disappeared by contemporary political terror elsewhere in Europe's former colonies as to the sedimented histories of those lost at sea in the 'Middle Passage, as global capitalism's constitutive act' (ibid.). In a line powerfully reminiscent of Derek Walcott's famous poem, 'The Sea is History', Brager insists, 'The water is full of evidence, and that which is dumped as trash reemerges to haunt us, demanding justice' (ibid.).

DOI: 10.1057/9781137444646.0007

Even as the bodies of Yaguine Koïta and Fodé Tounkara vanished among the legions of the lost and disappeared, their voices returned to circulate, through their carefully preserved letter, the traces of a call for justice. A deliberate and closely crafted document, the letter survives as a type of insurance for members of those classes that Brager terms 'prone to vanishing'. Preparing for the likely eventuality of their death and rapid disposal, the boys are determined not to die nameless or in silence. At once apologia and manifesto, their lucid articulation of the violent neocolonial and postcolonial geographies that entrap them, and of the aspirations of others like themselves to which they sought to draw attention, boldly claims the space to make its case, to articulate the call for justice in the face of a necropolitical order that seeks their disappearance.

Unlike the boys' fragile, contraband bodies, all too apt to disappear, the eloquent witness of their letter succeeded, fleetingly, in breaking through the silence and separation of the border. It drew global, if short-lived, attention to their dreams of flight. Reminiscent of a message in a bottle, the boys' letter is an attempt to communicate across a vast divide and against the odds: survival media.

Recalling the title of a hit track by the hip-hop artist M.I.A., I read Yaguine and Fodé's letter to the masters of Europe also as a kind of paper plane, an improvised and fugitive craft of dreams. In 'Paper Planes', as elsewhere in her work, M.I.A. draws on her own history as a child refugee from Lanka. Her provocative lyrics allude to the complex geographies of mobility, transgression and blockage within which refugee and migrant bodies must operate, and the subterranean and illegalised flights of creativity and mobility they engender. In the circuitous cartographies they inscribe over land and sea, the new itineraries they map in the air, illegalised and migrant subjects draw upon and adapt a panoply of media, among them their own bodies, as they cast themselves out from the known into new lives and spaces. Medium and message, mediating and mediated, these expressive and embodied lines of flight in turn invest the scenes and elements through which they move with new meanings and ontologies; they set in play new geographies, poetics and politics, new vectors of movement. These precarious transmutations and forced improvisations are the survival media of illegalised refugees and migrants. Survival media include forms of cultural politics, corporeal poetics and their material effects. Through their embodied and expressive movements, refugee and migrant bodies inscribe lines of flight that glide and float,

DOI: 10.1057/9781137444646.0007

coast and soar, even as they are ensnared in the lethal operations and entrapping force of the borders they seek to navigate.

Joseph Pugliese has discussed how state agencies deploy an array of everyday technologies and civic spaces as means of covert imprisonment and punishment for illegalised migrants, and transmute 'seemingly neutral and benign civil technologies' into 'modes of refugee trauma and death'. The targets of such practices at the same time redeploy 'these same civil technologies and objects (a shipping container for example)', a leaky wooden boat, a metal cavity as modes of escape and survival (2011, 143). Their passages and blockages, makeshift way stations and covert meeting points, map improbable itineraries, eke spaces for movement out of rock and razor wire. Following from Arjun Appadurai's theorisation of the imagination as an 'organized field of social practices... [that] is now central to all forms of agency, is itself a social fact, and is the key component of the new global order' (2003, 30), refugees and illegalised migrants are understood as 'imagineers' of multiple forms and modalities of flight and fancy that are at once forms of agency and 'social fact'. As imagineers, fugitive and illegalised migrants re-engineer and recast the material objects, spaces, cultural ecologies and 'social facts' through which they move.

Flying like paper

Along with the letter written by Yaguine Koïta and Fodé Tounkara, Belgian officials found several other pieces of paper alongside their bodies—birth certificates, school reports, family photographs—all assembled carefully in plastic bags. These, too, are potent media that protect, credential and authorise the refugee: paper planes that have the power to transport them to new lives. 'Where aspiration, even survival, is closely tied to the capacity to migrate,' Jean Comaroff and John Comaroff observe, papers 'take on a magic of their own'. At sites where 'human identities congeal along borders in paper and plastic', passports, visas, marriage and death certificates, degrees, security clearances, family trees and birth lines carry talismanic properties, spelling out the lines that demarcate freedom and imprisonment, life and death. In these places, papers, actual and symbolic, forged and authentic, are literally survival media. The techniques and manufacture of these vital counterfeits thus 'command a compelling power and fascination, rendering forgery a form

DOI: 10.1057/9781137444646.0007

of creativity that transcends easy definitions of legality' (Comaroff and Comaroff 2006, 12).

'I fly like paper, get high like planes/If you catch me at the border, I got visas in my name', the Tamil hip-hop artist M.I.A. ('Missing in Action') sings in 'Paper Planes'. The track, featured in the hit film *Slumdog Millionaire* (2007), brought a whole new audience to the music of M.I.A., the persona adopted by Maya Mathangi Arulpragasam, who had come to England with her mother as a child refugee from Lanka (see Chapter 2). If Danny Boyle's film provides an accomplished and ultimately reassuring fable of success for the homeless and impoverished third world child, a success story that M.I.A.'s own real-life story parallels, the lyrics of 'Paper Planes' follow the trajectory of the illegalised migrant as irredeemably suspect—criminal, forger, people smuggler, suspected murderer and possible terrorist. The music video for the track begins with shots of low-flying aircraft, a bold allusion to the 9/11 terror attacks. It is accompanied by a sound track of cash registers and gunshots, the shrieking of fax machines and cell phones, referencing the techno-hustles and backroom industries by which counterfeit visas are produced for unknown purposes. Like the 'inspired captains of fakery' described by Comaroff and Comaroff (2006, 12), the migrant as trickster, fraudster and forger of paper planes is the figure of a global folk outlaw, operating in the techno-underground and the cracks of the cyber economy to enable new mobilities across constrictive geographies and barred national borders.

Hand in hand with the deserving migrant and good refugee, the gangster, the criminal and the terrorist shadow the borders of the global north, troubling its claims to secure and sovereign nationhood. The dynamics of threat and fear they embody were strikingly exemplified in the narrative of a second boat carrying asylum seekers from Lanka to Australia, the KM *Jeya Lestari 5*, one of a scattered flotilla that put out to sea after the end of the war. Crammed on board were 254 people, some of whom had been waiting for asylum in detention camps in Indonesia or Malaysia for several years. One hundred and nine of them were already UNHCR certified refugees. They included a number of families, many with young children. When the boat was intercepted at Australia's request off the Indonesian port of Merak, a long and arduous stand-off ensued. The *Jeya Lestari*, which had represented a passage to freedom, now turned into a makeshift detention camp. As the passengers collectively refused to disembark, under siege from both Indonesian and

DOI: 10.1057/9781137444646.0007

Australian governments, their health and morale visibly deteriorated in the intolerable conditions. The Lankan government, too, sought to intervene, attacking the credibility of those on board, casting them as fraudsters, criminals and terrorists. The International Organization for Migration (IOM), the body responsible for overseeing welfare and assistance to asylum seekers, withdrew after initially providing food and medicine. Aboard the floating prison boat, exhaustion and illness began to take their toll. There were hunger strikes and threats of self-harm, coupled with mounting signs of tension between different groups on board, while some quietly jumped ship to return to Indonesia, hoping to set sail again another day.

During this period, a nine-year-old girl, Brindha, together with a man in his 20s, 'Alex', acted as the main spokespeople for those on board. Brindha captured the headlines when she made a direct appeal on-camera to the Australian public: 'Please help us and save our lives. We are your children. Please think of us, please, please' (Grattan and Allard 2009). The striking and charismatic 'Alex', whose real name was later revealed to be Sanjeev Kuhendrarajah, was a far more complex figure. It gradually emerged that Sanjeev was the son of Tamil diasporic parents who were citizens of Canada. Deemed an unfit non-citizen in Canada after a stint in prison for being a member of the Toronto Tamil street gang, Alex was deported to Lanka, and made his way to India before he, yet again, sought asylum by boarding the *Jeya Lestari* (Fitzpatrick 2009). In a series of performance-lectures on 'Alex' the Tamil-Australian artist, Sumugan Sivanesan, reflects, in the context of the commonalities they share as young diaspora Tamil men, on the identities and narratives demanded of the refugee, setting out to explore whether 'a flawed and...somewhat undesirable non-citizen, might yet determine a politics of mobility that has implications beyond his own self-interest' (2013, 132).

In Alex's tortuous movements—his to-ing and fro-ing and doublings back across Lanka, Canada, India, Malaysia, Indonesia and Thailand—and his multiple assumed and real identities—gang member, Indian call centre worker, member of the LTTE's Toronto wing, and most recently, Christian convert in the Thai jail where he is incarcerated, despite being a UN-recognised refugee—are the traces of an exuberant and improvisatory embodied repertoire. Coupled with the flamboyant hyper-masculinity of his self-presentations, evidenced in the selfies posted on his Facebook page, the various personae adopted by Sanjeev/Alex inhabit the same ambiguous spaces as the characters who flit through 'Paper

DOI: 10.1057/9781137444646.0007

Planes': the seamy and violent world of the migrant/refugee as hustler, gangster, criminal and possible terrorist. As in M.I.A.'s early productions, to some audiences, these personae retain something of the romance of the guerrilla that attached to the LTTE in its early years.

Sivanesan's performance-lectures are an attempt to connect the underworld of Sanjeev/Alex's ambivalent simulations as a 'captain of fakery' with the mixed-media of Sivanesan's own performances. At the intersection of artistic-academic practice and the performances of Sanjeev/Alex's multiple biographies, Sivanesan claims a space for their shared political investments in undoing the violent policing of borders and the interdictions that govern the bodies of refugees. Transposed from his performances aboard the *Jeya Lestari* to the space of the gallery and lecture theatre through the mediating figure of Sivanesan as artist, the persona of 'Alex', Sivanesan argues, may function at least fleetingly to 'cut through political manoeuvring and obfuscation and transform social relations between citizens and non-citizens' (2013, 139). In a later series of performances, Sivanesan seeks to transport both 'Alex' as art/artefact, and (via Skype) Sanjeev, as embodied presence in his Thailand jail, into the intersecting spaces of academia, art and activism. As survival media, the exchanges between Sivanesan and Sanjeev/Alex mediate—and are re-mediated across—geographical, cultural and virtual spaces, and scenes of freedom and confinement: boat, prison, gallery. The trajectories and vanishing points of these lines of flight remain always uneven, volatile and potentially lethal. Sanjeev's posting on Facebook of a selfie from jail reportedly resulted in his being beaten in his cell and the confiscation of his phone, a reminder of the violent and unequal conditions under which survival media operate.

Survival media as active repertoires of actions and changeable artefacts do not transcend conditions of confinement and blockage, but produce their own provisional spaces in and through them. Their vanishing points cannot exclude the possibility of the subject's own disappearance and death. In this sense, they echo Jayna Brown's insistence on the 'necessity to recognize [that] the utopian new moments of global connection and diasporic formation', such as Sivanesan's performances and the enabling conditions of M.I.A's music, take place within irredeemably 'necropolitical worlds': spaces of terror and death, of endless border wars and desperate poverty, of detention camps and jail boats, peopled by child soldiers, and stateless refugees. Brown argues that what distinguishes these media is the impulse to 'improvise on the refuse of

DOI: 10.1057/9781137444646.0007

destruction', even as the expressive forms and possibilities of the music and dance produced in these conditions remain 'momentary, ephemeral and elusive' (2010, 127–8). Brown's insistence on the doubleness of this state, on the improvisational and creative energies it harnesses, as well as on the materialities that ground it in rubble, waste, disappearance and death, with both elements held in a present animated by intimations of the past and the future, resonates with Jasbir Puar's description of a 'critical creative politics' of 'anticipatory temporalities'. This is a state, Puar writes, where 'the becoming future is haunting us—while its ontological debt to that which once was nevertheless cautions us' (2000, xx).

Subject to vanishing: departures, dispersals, disposals

In the form of the invisible pull on a rope under water, an unaccountable drift of ashes in the still air, the freight of that 'ontological debt to that which once was', attends subjects in flight. The oceans over which they sail, and in which they drown or fall prey to sharks, are not only a capricious, unknowable surface, but composed of a multitude of historical currents and flows, constituted by sedimented layers, by spectral genealogies, iconographies and epistemologies. A caution on the future and a beckoning from the past, they carry the insoluble remnants of the lost and disappeared, traces of other forced passages and trafficked bodies, set in motion by the forces of empire's violence.

One of the most plangent, evocative accounts of the dispersal from Lanka is an autobiographical essay by the Indian novelist, Amitav Ghosh. Ghosh spent much of his childhood in Lanka, his 'Serendib before the fall' (2003, 1). Ghosh's meditation on narratives of departure and arrival, exodus and dispersal, distinguishes between the forward-moving gaze of migrants arriving in North America and the lingering backwards gaze of diaspora Lankan authors such as Michael Ondaatje and Shyam Selvadurai. The gaze of departure is exemplified for Ghosh in the closing scene of Selvadurai's novel, *Funny Boy*, and the narrator's final backwards look at the ashes of his house consumed in the conflagrations of Black July.

In contrast to the trajectories of hopeful arrival that shape narratives of exodus, for Ghosh, are the non-teleological movements of dispersal, where there is no sense of an overarching historical or providential design. Instead, a random and banal violence, sanctioned or perpetrated

DOI: 10.1057/9781137444646.0007

by the state, directs the wanderings of the dispersed: 'This is where recollection turns its back on history, for it is the burden of history to make sense of the past, while the memory of dispersal is haunted always by the essential inexplicability of what has come to pass; by the knowledge that there was nothing inevitable, nothing predestined about what has happened' (2003, 3). If exodus and dispersal are not always so clearly distinguishable, what Ghosh acutely pinpoints nonetheless is the abiding sense of loss and breakdown engendered by ateleological and random movements of dispersal, the scattering caused by the collapse of any possibility of an ethical relation between state and subject: a 'species of pain', exactly, that 'runs so poignantly through the literature that resulted from the Partition of the Indian subcontinent in 1947' (ibid., 4).

The gash of partition, as a 'species of pain' that severs citizen from citizen, and subject from nation, produces a profound unmooring and ontological dislocation. In Channa Wickremesekera's *In the Same Boat*, a tale of Lankan asylum seekers en route to Australia, the sight of a boat inexplicably in flames in mid-ocean invokes both the wreck of the ship of state and the plight of its subjects left adrift, all at sea:

> What could be burning in the middle of the sea, somebody asked…In a few minutes they could see the boat too, a blue fishing trawler drifting out on the sea with flames lazily licking the sides of what had been its cabin, as if it had all the time in the world to consume it…
>
> Everyone kept looking as their boat passed the burning vessel, slowly, as if in slow motion. The smoke from the fire wafted around them, stinging their eyes and breath. On the deck of the blue trawler no one could be seen.
>
> How could it have happened, someone asked, softly, almost fearfully.
>
> No one answered. (2012, 41)

This scene of a burning boat registers the multiple forms of violence to which bodies in flight are only too prone. Those on board, as fugitive citizens 'in the same boat', confront the image of the ship of state slowly consumed by its own violence. In this scene between fire and water, past and future merge into an intolerable, irresolvable, yet persistent, question: 'How could it have happened?' This is a question that returns again and again in variant forms as a recurring burden of the diasporic productions discussed in later chapters.

The postcolonial violence of partition and its aftermath form a long continuum: the flows of empire and capital, and the relentless swell and drag of bodies to the edges of the global north. The missing and

DOI: 10.1057/9781137444646.0007

disappeared bodies of the burning boat are linked through Brager's 'genealogies of violence' to other bodies on the run, and to yet other expendable, invisible bodies hidden under the waves. As a freight that both weighs down and drives forward, these remains and their hauntings carry the spectres and avenging spirits of the undead, as well as the burden of a call to justice across borders and for the future, for, as Brager points out, 'the ritual of body disposal, which prevents or makes ghosts, is at the foundation of political community' (2015).

Returns

The refugee boat, as an ambiguous artefact of mobility and survival, rides the currents of freedom and unfreedom, life and death, stasis and flow. In Merak Harbour, following nine-year-old Brindha's televised appeal to the Australian public, access to the *Jaya Lestari 5* was restricted, and an exclusion zone imposed to prevent contact with reporters. Its passengers did not remain passive or silent in response to this attempt to immobilise them. Like the bodies dumped in the sea as waste, the wreckage of a necropolitical order, the flotsam and jetsam of the surrounding waters were pressed into service as survival media for subjects in flight: scraps of paper, plastic bags and castaway bottles found new uses, resignified in the movement of waves and the drift of waters. Communication with assembled news crews and activists continued, now through the means of messages in English and Indonesian written on torn off pieces of paper, rolled up inside plastic bags and tied to empty plastic water bottles before being tossed into the sea. One of these messages, from the *Jaya Lestari*'s companion boat, the *Oceanic Viking*, was retrieved by Australian reporters. Reminiscent of the letter written by Yaguine Koïta and Fodé Tounkara, it spoke not in the voice of the supplicant or victim, but through a direct claiming of rights and subject positions: 'Until now we heard that your country is a humanitarian country and also the refugee can restart their new life with freedom in your country' (Kearney 2009). As it succinctly articulated an ethical demand for protection, the message called into question the self-representations of the receiving nation.

Through this terse but pointed effort to break out of the state of physical and communicative immobilisation imposed on the *Oceanic Viking* and the *Jaya Lestari*, the message in a bottle, the stuff of the shipwreck

DOI: 10.1057/9781137444646.0007

dramas and castaway plots so central to the western literary tradition, stages its unexpected return (see Chapter 3). As an image out of time, the message in a bottle signifies in the present as the sign of a romantic or quixotic gesture. Yet returned to the context of the sea and its dangers, the message in a bottle takes the form of a solicitation. Caught in the random movement of currents, carried on the roll and thrust of waves, the message in a bottle is predicated on the belief in an exchange to come, a compact that remains to be fulfilled between shore and sea, writer and reader, sender and addressee. The message in a bottle carries across a gulf that is both ethical and spatial, across an ocean that has been rendered a space of terror, to claim a bond between host and arrival, citizen and refugee.

I end by returning to the *Bremen*, the boat with which the chapter began. In September 2014, the Western Australian Museum announced that, after almost a year of being impounded, the boat would become part of Western Australia's display of maritime heritage. Those who had arrived aboard it had been long dispersed: some were returned to Lanka under a program of 'enhanced screening', an Orwellian name which concealed their summary deportation to an unknown fate; others were consigned to indefinite detention in offshore gulags where they were deliberately exposed to harsh and punitive conditions.

The decision to preserve the *Bremen* was a break with the long-established practice of burning asylum boats, described by one journalist as the 'torching rite' of Australian sovereignty (Hernandez 2012). Torching is the regular treatment meted out to vessels deemed to have breached the indeterminate border zone between Australia and Indonesia. The burning vessel that the asylum seekers of *In the Same Boat* contemplate with such horror is a reference to this practice. The historian Ruth Balint reported that in Darwin in the early 2000s, the burning of boats used by Indonesian fishers from the island of Roti was 'a public spectacle, and onlookers have been known to drape themselves in and wave Australian flags enthusiastically as the *prau* explode in flames' (Balint 2005, 98). The eventual destruction of the asylum boat, as Sean Anderson and Jennifer Ferng write, concludes the 'closed cycle of naval patrol, processing and detention, leaving no tangible proof of the long journey taken between countries' (2013, 217).

If the destruction of the asylum-seeker' boat obliterates the 'tangible proof' of their voyage and arrival, a staging of the sovereign power over those classes who are prone to vanishing, how do we understand

DOI: 10.1057/9781137444646.0007

the fate of the *Bremen*, reprieved from the flames and transferred to the confines of a state museum? High and dry, does it signify, perhaps, as a trophy of sovereign power, reaffirming the insular nation, Fortress Australia? Incorporated into a narrative of national maritime history, does it collude in the erasure of those who sailed aboard it, consigned now to an unknown fate? I want to believe that, like other artefacts assembled in the space of the museum, the meanings and resonances of the *Bremen* may not be so easily contained. With its jaunty trim, its hopeful flag, this survivor of oceans speaks to me also of the long, fear-filled nights and days of the voyage out, of the hopeful swell and roll of waves, of tides receding yet returning, and, amidst the churning of stomachs and hearts, of an irrepressible billowing and beckoning, and the flash of makeshift stars: *in flight*.

DOI: 10.1057/9781137444646.0007

2
Missing in Action: By All Media Necessary

Abstract: *Chapter 2 discusses the cultural and biographical productions of hip-hop artist M.I.A. (Maya Arulpragasam), described as 'the most famous member of the Tamil diaspora'. It suggests that 'missing in action' is also a framework for understanding diasporic subjectivities and histories of war and conflict.*

Keywords: Born Free; M.I.A; Maya Arulpragasam; methodology of the oppressed; Missing in Action; Tamil hip-hop

Perera, Suvendrini. *Survival Media: The Politics and Poetics of Mobility and the War in Sri Lanka.* New York: Palgrave Macmillan, 2016. DOI: 10.1057/9781137444646.0008.

In 2009, as the formal war in Lanka was nearing its grim conclusion, a report in the *New York Times* described Mathangi 'Maya' Arulpragasam, who had become familiar to millions across the globe in her persona as the hip-hop performer, M.I.A.—for 'Missing in Action'—as the 'most famous member of the Tamil diaspora' (Mackey 2009). In the last weeks of the war, M.I.A made a number of public appeals on behalf of those trapped by the fighting, including a last-minute tweet entreating an intervention by Oprah Winfrey. The appeal, which went unheeded, was ill-judged and inspired in equal parts. It suggests the uncertain, precarious terrain that M.I.A. treads: teetering between triviality and trauma, yoking popular culture to geopolitics, trading the hypervisibility of the media-celebrity circuit against the faceless desperation of lives abandoned by governments and global institutions alike.

In addition to being nominated for an Academy Award and two Grammys, M.I.A. was named on *Esquire* magazine's list of the 75 most influential people of the twenty-first century and on *Time*'s annual *Time 100* list for 2009, indicating a level of public significance that exceeds the reach of her music alone. In January 2009, in the final months of the war, she appeared on Tavis Smiley's influential talk show on US public television:

SMILEY: My time with you is up. Will you indulge me just one time? I want to hear you say your full name. Just say it for me one time, your full name.
M.I.A.: It's Mathangi 'Maya' Arulpragasam.
SMILEY: I just wanted to hear that. That's all. (Laughter) I knew I never could. I'll just call her M.I.A.
M.I.A.: It's a Tamil thing.
SMILEY: Yeah, it's a Tamil thing. (Smiley 2009)

In this chapter, I consider the transformation of Mathangi 'Maya' Arulpragasam into M.I.A., Missing in Action, as a Tamil thing, an emblematic diaspora story. The narrative weaves itself, uneasily, improbably, around the figure of M.I.A., threading fragments of memory, music, cultural politics and history into its fabric of violence and survival, presence and absence, resistance and complicity, loss and self-making. Its driving questions are about the impossible choices, willed identifications, ethical and emotional imperatives which present themselves in a dirty war, a war in which both sides are mired in brutal violence; a war experienced as at once remote and intimate. It explores the forms of creativity they engender, in their inescapable traces and unaccountable hauntings and returns in diasporic lives. In particular, it focuses on M.I.A.'s practice of an embodied

DOI: 10.1057/9781137444646.0008

poetics that expresses the contradictory affective and political investments, shifting positionalities, and conflicting solidarities of diaspora lives.

Missing in Action is a name that speaks a whole history of loss, damage and pain in a war where no clear distinction separates military from civilian casualties. A term that attests to the military desire for order, Missing in Action designates that which is not to be found in the theatre of war, but that still remains within it, through the very naming of its non-presence. Missing in Action classifies someone whose body cannot be located either on a battlefield or outside it. It may signify the unburied or undead, as well as the fighter held captive or who has given up the battle; it encompasses the untraceable and the disappeared, the absconder and the escapee. Missing in Action is a paradox that attempts to assign a fixed status to an unknown state; it is precise yet indeterminable, situated yet unfixed, provisional yet capable of indefinite extension.

As a figure for 'a Tamil thing', Missing in Action invokes the gone-missing, the here and not-here of the diasporic. Missing in Action is a state reminiscent of amputation, the part of a whole that is not to be found, yet is still deeply felt: present in the gash and ache of loss. To be Missing in Action may still hint at being 'in action' elsewhere: to remain active while being missing; to be active and present in one place while being missing or absent from another. In this sense, it is a state that speaks not only of vacancy and loss, but also of participation or engagement, through both presence and absence, in more than one location.

The grim events of the war's end in Lanka form part of a much older, continuing, asymmetrical narrative of terror and mass slaughter where violence piles upon violence, a lethal accumulation of historical acts that continues to ramify and repeat through ever-widening circles of reception, in the type of deadly exchange that Robert Young describes as a 'dialectic without transcendence':

> First, there is the act, which achieves impact, destruction, maiming, death. And then, ever more, violence operates as a kind of haunting: Sethe waiting for her Beloved's ghostly return in Toni Morrison's novel, the state still haunted by its own former fury, the torturer possessed by his victim's ghostly faces. But the victim is haunted too, can remember the face, still hears the voice, echoing in her sleep, preventing peace.

> And even those who have only lived it imaginatively... cannot get away from its lingering whispers... Our lives, however tranquil, remain haunted by its insistent spectral repetitions, some visible, and others secret, by its tortured interruptions. (2009, 4)

DOI: 10.1057/9781137444646.0008

How do such spectral repetitions and tortured interruptions of a violence that is both distant, in space or time, and deeply connected, both public and secret, resurface in unannounced, recomposed forms, among youthful diaspora groups? What are the expressive and cultural forms in which they re-appear or re-sound, sometimes when least expected? How do they address, and how are they received by, multiple audiences, both those intimately possessed by its memories and those who have lived it at many removes, yet cannot escape its 'lingering whispers'—the whispers relayed in family stories or historical events that continue to resonate through the decades, in fragments of verse or echoes of song, the flash of images from a news story on television? A blank-faced child holding a rifle in its hands, a tiger poised to spring, a ruined house of many rooms, a bus trip to nowhere, a field of slaughter: these are the hidden tracks and obscured traces that, figured forth through the elusive sign, Missing In Action, stitch this chapter together.

A wrath-bearing tree

But this narrative of presences, absences and returns, of multiple names and locations, of fixed yet unfixable positions, begins somewhere else, with someone I'll call Peter, an escapee from another intractable war. Peter spent much of his teenage and young adult years in a refugee camp in Africa before arriving in Australia. He is guarded in his first conversations with me until I mention that I am a Tamil from Sri Lanka and can guess at some of the more unspeakable aspects of life in uncivil war zones. 'Oh, I thought you were from South America', he says. Before I can elaborate on the determinants and choices that mark a Tamil-Lankan-Australian woman with a name familiar in both South America and South Asia, but originating in an obscure corner of imperial Europe, he starts to tell me a different story—though this, too, is a story of the strange circulations and the violent, unaccountable trajectories of names.

He says that during his childhood, about which I suppose a lot, but know almost nothing, he often heard the commander in a certain rebel army exhort his troops to be 'strong like the Tamil Tigers'. Peter had no idea who the Tamil Tigers were, or where they came from, but he remembered those stories about them after he had escaped from this war, found his way to a refugee camp and was able to go to school again. During his years of growing up in the frightening and famishing conditions of a

DOI: 10.1057/9781137444646.0008

vast refugee camp, Peter somehow made the time to find Sri Lanka on a map and to learn what he could about the war there: about the Tamils, and those fighters—the legendary Tigers—who were held up to him as models during his own years in a battle zone somewhere in Africa.

Peter's flash of memory makes a tenuous and yet palpable bond between him and me, though I have never fought in a battle, or lived in a refugee camp. His story stayed with me for days. The circle of hungry, frightened boys; a hidden camp. A commander who captures the imagination with a single name, as he holds these small bodies hostage with weapons and blows and starvation. Be strong, be like the Tamil Tigers. The global reach of this name kept coming back to me as the Tigers' final military defeat, something that had once seemed unachievable, took shape on my TV screen. I wept for Peter, and children like him, and also for something else, something hidden and suspect: some trace or buried vibration that I found difficult to name.

The stages of the LTTE's defeat in May 2009, as the Lankan army engaged in murderous, indiscriminate shelling, were measured by the painful passage of refugees out of the war zone. Ragged, emaciated, wounded, broken, they emerged into camera view in their thousands. Some bore bundles or tattered bags over their heads as they waded across the lagoon into government territory. Others held stained grey rags tied to the ends of twigs, frail messages of surrender. A man shaking with sobs carries the still form of a dead child in his arms. Unforgettable, the droop of her small head, hair in neatly doubled-up plaits, falling over his arm.

On 17 May 2009, the LTTE officially announced that its 30-year war against the Lankan state had reached its 'bitter end' (Reuters 2009). I spent the night, like thousands of others in all quarters of the globe, in a state of restless agitation, obsessively searching websites for news, sifting and relaying rumours, fearing and doubting, reflecting, remembering. That night I understood, perhaps for the first time, that although it has not struck me with the same direct and ferocious violence that so many have experienced, this war is the determining factor of my life. The war is the unseen horizon of my actions and options, it provides the bare coordinates that locate me, my store of identifications, memories and stories— even those that pre-date its own chronological beginning. Though I am not a refugee, this war placed me where I am, as it has most of my family, my oldest friends, and more than a million unknown others with whom I share little but this one intractable, brute fate: the war.

DOI: 10.1057/9781137444646.0008

Peter's recollections stirred something in my memory, old talk of daring exploits and audacious improvisations on unequal ground. These long ago, long gone visions of guerrilla resistance and liberation once inspired thousands, as Tamils faced both systemic discrimination and eruptions of direct pogrom-type violence orchestrated by the state. Girls and boys left home to train in jungle camps, some with the blessing of their parents, while others stole away in silence. A whole university entrance class from an elite Jaffna school, it is said, walked out of the classroom one day to enlist en masse. The people of Jaffna forgot their legendary thrift to invest in hope: sold jewellery and land to buy into the nation fantasy, caught up in the energies of this heady period.

During the early 1980s, the various groups of young militants who took up arms in the cause of Tamil separatism were known simply as 'the boys', as if they were the neighbourhood cricket team or part of an extended family of cousins. What happened to this family relationship has been carefully detailed elsewhere. Sometime during the ensuing years, as the demand for justice turned to unreflexive violence, and national aspirations into Tigerism, the myriad Tamil liberation movements that had sprouted in the 1980s were crushed one by one by the LTTE (Manikkalingam 1995). The relationship between the people and 'the boys' inverted, bent violently out of shape. Sumathy writes:

> The people, Tamils here, rendered passive and static, congeal into the object of the struggle; they are only an end, not the means. They are only to be delivered, not the deliverers…defined into a hegemonic oneness; the Tamil people, the Tamil cause, the nation. All actors, distinct from the object then neatly fall into the camp of the liberator/representative or that of the traitor/sell out. (2001, 2–3)

As the LTTE's internal violence escalated, naming the multiple forms of oppression experienced by the people of Jaffna became an act of extraordinary courage. The authors of the remarkable volume, *Broken Palmyra*, faced extreme intimidation and violence (Hoole et al. 1990). The growing opposition or ambivalence many Tamils felt towards the LTTE and other militant separatists was offset as well by the vocal support of others who took pride in the fact that Tamils, stereotyped as given to book-learning and bureaucracy rather than to sport or war, were at last fighting back. While internal unease and opposition towards the LTTE, though brutally suppressed, continued to manifest themselves among the Tamils of the north, the LTTE's militancy was buttressed by substantial financial and emotional backing from diaspora groups who largely ignored or denied

DOI: 10.1057/9781137444646.0008

the internal violence perpetrated by the LTTE because of a focus on the greater violence perpetrated by the state.

Liberators and people, actors and acted on: for Tamil militancy the logic of that violent relationship culminated more than 20 years later on a shrinking sliver of ground, a narrow sand spit between ocean and lagoon, at the very edges of the Jaffna peninsula in the obscure hamlet of Mullivaikkal. At this extremity of the territory they had once controlled, LTTE fighters, accompanied by both their last-ditch supporters and those they had terrorised into compliance, were brutally shelled and pounded into surrender by a state that had adopted the tactics of a guerrilla army, while shrewdly deploying the rhetoric of the global war on terror.

That night, lacking words, I emailed some half-remembered lines to a friend in Colombo who had lived through the war, and on whom it had inflicted painful wounds.

> Think
> Neither fear nor courage saves us. Unnatural vices
> Are fathered by our heroism. Virtues
> Are forced upon us by our impudent crimes.
> These tears are shaken from the wrath-bearing tree.
> The tiger springs in the new year. Us he devours.

(T.S. Eliot, 'Gerontian' 1920 [1971], 21)

The lines were from a poem by T.S. Eliot that I had hated, but not forgotten, since the days I first read it in the tin shed, hastily slapped down in the middle of a former coconut estate, that served as the English department of our branch of the University of Sri Lanka. My friend emailed back immediately, also surprised: 'I had not thought Eliot could be so evocative'.

> Think now
> History has many cunning passages, contrived corridors
> And issues, deceives with whispering ambitions,
> Guides us by vanities.
> ...Gives too late
> What's not believed in, or if still believed,
> In memory only, reconsidered passion. Gives too soon
> Into weak hands, what's thought can be dispensed with
> Till the refusal propagates a fear.

(ibid.)

Wrenched from their context of Christian apocalypse, the lines carried a surge of powerful associations. If the figure of the tiger symbolised Christ's transformative power for Eliot, the Tiger spoke to us of the lethal

DOI: 10.1057/9781137444646.0008

delusions of the nation fantasy, as it melds the heroic into the criminal, strength into murderous weakness, conviction into hatred.

Since the last days of the war, refugees have streamed out of Lanka, selling what little they owned, borrowing and promising and lying to get on planes or cast themselves away in small boats, fleeing the 'welfare villages' and barbed wire camps set up to hold them, the devastation of the war zone and the vindictive, triumphal ethnonationalism of the state. Their stories, too, emerge in Gerontian's reflections on the aftermath of war and the dispersal of peoples. They speak through Eliot's racist, anti-Semitic, old-man voice, with its thick revulsion for the foreigner. In the years when Eliot was writing 'Gerontian', refugees from the revolution in Russia and the collapsing Ottoman empire were finding their way into Europe. They included Armenian survivors of the 1915 genocide in Turkey, White Russians fleeing the Bolsheviks, and Jewish refugees from the greater Caucasus. Gerontian's rage at a Europe turned into a rented house, occupied by shabby, promiscuous, polyglot tenants, is one that returns, as if for the first time, a century later, after the brief interregnum of European humanitarianism engendered by the disclosure of the Nazi genocides. Gerontian's concentrated disgust for the refugee as a figure of the cosmopolitan, the racial interloper in the house of European high culture, is only too recognisable in the fortress Europe of the twenty-first century. This Europe made over by the unruly presence of refugees and survivors, a raucous, motley, hungry people on the move, is the ground from which M.I.A.'s music, with its fierce kinetic energies, its irrepressible defiance, its multiform challenges to the established order, resounds, at once joyous and discordant.

Tenants of the house

M.I.A. was born on 18 July 1975 in London. According to an account in the *Guardian*, her parents had met in a pub in Hounslow:

> Arul, her father, had landed a scholarship to learn engineering in Russia when he was 15, after which he came to London; Kala was studying for a few months... [and] needed to extend her visa, Arul agreed to marry her, and did so, in a matter of days. They had two girls in two years...But unknown to Kala, Arul had become involved with some politically minded Tamils, and, when Maya was two months old, he left. 'He went out to buy a pint of milk and didn't come back for four months,' says Maya. 'He went to Lebanon. To train with the PLO.' (Sawyer 2010)

DOI: 10.1057/9781137444646.0008

The early years of Tamil militancy were inflected by the spectrum of liberation movements of the 1960s and 1970s: civil rights and Black nationalism in the United States, ideologies of Cuban and Latin American revolution, anti-colonial struggles in Angola, Rhodesia and South Africa, and especially, increasing Palestinian resistance throughout the Middle East. These combined with regional energies of the rise of Tamil consciousness in South India through the *Dravida Munnetra Kazakam* (DMK). When M.I.A.'s father returned from his training in Lebanon, the whole family moved to Jaffna, the Tamil capital in northern Lanka, where Arul became a founding member of EROS (Eelam Revolutionary Organization of Students), taking the *nom de guerre* Arular. Like many young men in Jaffna in these years of growing support for militant Tamil separatism, he left his family to go underground soon after.

M.I.A.'s first album, *Arular* (2005) is often taken as a direct tribute to this absent fighter-father figure, but M.I.A. sometimes puts forward a more complicated genealogy of diasporic survival: 'Everyone thinks my story is to do with my dad, when, you know, it's my uncle in Morden [south London] on my mother's side who's my inspiration…the first ever brown guy to have his own stall on Petticoat Lane'.

'Everywhere you look in Maya's vast family', the reporter comments, 'there's a story of adversity overcome, an epic adventure' (Sawyer 2010). The many epic stories of M.I.A.'s formation are characteristic of thousands of diasporic Tamil families in the last decades of the twentieth century. Following the 1983 pogroms of Black July, separatist militancy in the north rose dramatically. Tamils who had been directly targeted by the violence fled to camps in South India or, if they could manage it, to the United Kingdom, Canada and Australia, as well as to France, Norway and other European states. This was the second major diaspora of Tamil refugees, following a previous dispersal in 1958, after an earlier series of murderous pogroms.

Kala and her children fled the war in Jaffna in the early 1980s, living in South India before returning as refugees in 1986 to a council flat in London. The transformation of Mathangi 'Maya' Arulpragasam into M.I.A. invokes not only the 'Missing in Action' of being both inside and outside the war in Jaffna, but also of being 'Missing in *Acton*', in the dubious refuge that life in London provided in the years following the Brixton riots of 1981 (Empire 2005): 'We were one of the two Asian families that lived there. I used to come home from school and see people burgling my house, just walk past with my telly. But it wasn't as horrible as being in Sri Lanka' (Frere-Jones 2004).

DOI: 10.1057/9781137444646.0008

It was in Acton, after her radio was stolen, that Maya first heard the music of Public Enemy being played on it from a neighbouring flat. This Afro-American male voice from New York's mean streets was instantly recognisable to a teenage Tamil refugee girl in South London: 'Hip-hop was the first thing that made me feel like I belonged to something in England' (Shapiro 2005). Paradoxically, the sense of belonging engendered by hip-hop was one structured by exclusion: 'I was already used to that thinking, being a Tamil, a guerrilla. Hip-hop was the most guerrilla thing happening in England at the time. You had Public Enemy fronting it, and that felt like home, and I could dance while I was feeling shitty. It had a whole aesthetic to it—it was being really crass with pride' (Orlov 2005). Hip-hop's power was its ability to transform the states of abjection and dehumanisation that racism and xenophobia produced (the sense of 'being really crass'), into an energising corporeal poetics of pride, defiance and joy.

Hip-hop was speaking to other young post-1983 diaspora Tamils in the same terms, linking resistance to the experience of oppression in Lanka—being 'a Tamil, a guerrilla'—to solidarity against racism in their countries of refuge. Such moments recall an earlier instance in the trajectory of Tamil diasporics: In *A Different Hunger*, A. Sivanandan, the pioneering editor of the journal *Race & Class*, who arrived in London after the 1958 anti-Tamil pogroms, recalled the day when he first heard the voice of Paul Robeson, played on the radio of a small bakery in Jaffna whose owner spoke no English (1981). Just as Robeson's voice articulated persecution for a previous generation, hip-hop spoke to many young diaspora Tamils after 1983.The recollections of the performer and activist D'Lo closely reflect those of M.I.A.:

> In the 1980s a little Sri Lankan kid in Lancaster, California, had her eyes glued to the movie *Breakin'* when it aired on national television…She knew there was a war going on in her parents' homeland and the way her father spoke about it led her to compare it to the way Public Enemy spoke to Black folks…I know that she will always remember 'Ladies First' whenever she sees Queen Latifah on screen … [T]his Sri Lankan boy-girl from Lancaster ['Sri Lankaster'] California, remembers finally feeling powerful being born into a woman's body. (D'Lo 2008, 138)

Identification with hip-hop provides a way to articulate experiences of Tamil suffering that were invisible in the United States or Europe, while also forging broader solidarities with feminist, queer and anti-racist

DOI: 10.1057/9781137444646.0008

movements. D'Lo remembers: 'From a young age I respected hip-hop's place in Black culture, but I also came to realize that hip-hop had a central place in my own identity as a South Asian American' (D'Lo 2008, 138). Hip-hop provided a vocabulary, a cultural ethos and, most important, an embodied consciousness that enabled her to see 'the parallels between hip-hop as a voice of Black frustration and the struggles of my own people' (D'Lo 2008, 140).

Like M.I.A.'s acute awareness of growing up as a Tamil girl 'Missing in Action' in South London, D'Lo's life in 'Sri Lankaster', California, produced a powerful consciousness of the pervasive force and violence of whiteness, and an identification with nonwhite, coloured and black identities deeply informed by the anti-racist and Black nationalist roots of hip-hop: 'We danced and wrote and hip-hopped together because we had to stick together; we couldn't afford to be lost in a sea of White' (D'Lo 2008, 140). As Sujatha Fernandes points out, hip-hop 'has been both global and diasporic since its beginnings' (2011, 20). Robin Kelley notes that from its inception, hip-hop was marked by an 'incredible hybridity' that 'reflected the increasingly international character of America's inner cities' and the influx of mobile, inexpensive and easily adaptable global technologies (1997, 39).

Together with the formative rhythms of hip-hop and rap, M.I.A.'s music is shaped by the other sounds of immigrant and working-class London in the 1980s and 1990s—dancehall, reggae, punk, bhangra—combining with echoes of Tamil film songs. The title of her first single, 'Galang' (2003)—'London Calling / Speak the Slang now'—apparently refers to the Jamaicanisation of the quintessential Cockney expression, 'G'wan' (Absolute Lyrics, n.d.). Released by a small independent company, 'Galang' is a tale of the new Londoner's battle for survival. The video features M.I.A. rapping and dancing against a rapidly changing backdrop of graffiti on a crumbling London wall. The Tamil word எப்படி? (*how?*), repeated over and over, appears in vividly coloured, stylised letters behind her, while the stencil outline of a tiger on the prowl flashes on and off, lurking among coconut trees or poised in mid-spring, alongside generic mediatised glimpses of a war zone: tanks, helicopters, explosions. The shifting backdrop of graffiti connects the lyrics, with their uncompromising narrative of growing up rough on London's council estates (*they say... work is gonna save you / pray and you will pull through / suck a dick'll help you / don't let em get to you*) to the violence of a different war in another place. The dancer embodies the link between

DOI: 10.1057/9781137444646.0008

two worlds of violence, multiplying to fill the screen in formations that evoke guerrilla ranks as much as disco or Bollywood. At the end, the scene darkens with smoke or fog as the dancer, a solitary figure again, her face now hooded and invisible, body shrouded in a standard-issue ghetto hoodie, comes forward to graffiti the letters M.I.A. directly on to the camera lens.

Maya Arulpragasam's success as a hip-hop musician followed two previous false starts to her career: as an artist (she once won the Alternative Turner Prize) and a filmmaker. Both were based on her degree from the prestigious St. Martin's Art School in London, an institution to which, she has said, she gained admission only because she argued that her alternative would be to turn to prostitution. Like her music, Arulpragasam's art practice was crucially shaped by the cultural politics of Tamil militancy. The LTTE and its supporters and fellow-travellers successfully combined popular culture (concerts, CDs), everyday sociality (grocery shopping, cultural festivals) and new media technologies to produce an ideologically saturated diasporic environment. The LTTE's means of communicating with diaspora communities evolved from early forms of 'net-war' and VHS video newsletters circulated through Tamil grocery stores in cities such as London, Toronto or Melbourne in the early 1980s, to the establishment of its own TV station. M.I.A. describes how the early 'video newsletters', which always ended with photographs of LTTE fighters who had died in war, provided the impetus for the stencil images she created in art school and that would later appear on her early music videos and album covers:

> Copies of copies of copies. They were filled with glitches…with '80s-style video transitions and a few analog effects…The tapes always ended with a sequence of the Tigers who had been killed or reported Missing in Action…Maya photographed stills from the tapes from the TV screen and she blew up the images to make large prints…Faces of girls her age, frozen in a moment of video. (Loveridge in Arulpragasam 2012, 11)

These remediated images and narratives, 'copies of copies of copies', also came to serve another function after the global crackdown on terror groups post 9/11: 'The effects of 9/11 hit the Tamil people in a fucked up way. Soon these tapes were considered a terrorist material and were destroyed. Not only were the people in the videos dead, but their images were destroyed…To the future and the world, they didn't exist. I wanted to document the documents' (ibid., 18).

DOI: 10.1057/9781137444646.0008

The entwining of cultural, aesthetic and political, of documentary and creative projects with the autobiographical, is signalled in an interview shortly after her first hip-hop success:

> The week I graduated, I got a phone call that my cousin had just died in Sri Lanka. He was kind of my twin: we were the same age, same month…He joined the Tigers and he died…Then I got another word that he was still alive, but was brain-dead at some hospital. So I went to find him. It was my first trip back to Sri Lanka since I left, and being that I'd got a film degree, I wanted to make a film about it—called 'MIA'. It was hardcore, because pretty much everybody I met never had access to the press before…Yet I couldn't do anything with it cause it was Tamil. (Orlov 2005)

The cousin/twin missing in action, a stand-in for the Maya who went missing from the war zone, also stands for a larger loss: a generation of young women and men caught between indiscriminate state violence directed at Tamils in the north as potential terrorists, and the internal violence of the LTTE, which included intimidation, blackmail and forcible recruitment of boys and girls into their ranks.

> So a whole youth culture there had gone missing. I went there and filmed it. I wanted to make a young beautiful thing about what had happened to my cousin and to all my other cousins…Rather than make a youth culture film in England, it was going to be what a market-stall kid in Africa or India or Sri Lanka experiences today. (ibid.)

The 'hardcore' story of this lost generation of young Tamils might have succeeded in a different kind of London, in another era. Caught in the crude geopolitical binaries of the war on terror, where only two sides—in President George Bush's words, 'us' and 'the terrorists'—were recognisable, their story was impossible to tell (Bush 2001).

> When I brought 60 hours of footage back to England, 9/11 just happened and it was considered propaganda material for the Tamils, who are just considered blanket terrorists these days…So I took single frames from them and made them into disposable fashion-y wallpaper and stencils…It was bored and ugly. But it was done in pretty colors, so people didn't know what I was talking about. (Orlov 2005)

The stories Arulpragasam sought to tell did not bear translation in post 9/11 England. In this climate of suspicion and shut-down, marked by racial profiling at home, and rendition and secret torture sites abroad, her raw stories were rendered doubly invisible: not only silenced, but

DOI: 10.1057/9781137444646.0008

distorted beyond recognition: wrenched out of their settings, literally cut up and disjointed, as the war in Lanka is subsumed into the war on terror. The Tamil voices and bodies recorded on film become unintelligible and unrecognisable, transposed onto the static, disposable medium of wallpaper. In place of the 'young beautiful thing' Arulpragasam hoped to make, the process of transmutation from film to wallpaper is 'bored and ugly', yet done in pretty colours in an unsuccessful attempt to disguise the uncivil and bloody places from which they emerged.

Two failed artefacts—an unmade film and a ream of disposable wallpaper—precede the emergence of the hip-hop persona, M.I.A. Precisely as a hip-hop artefact, the persona M.I.A. recomposes a number of survival elements. A stand-in for a lost twin-self and a generation gone missing, it projects both absence and presence, embodying a link between those lost, here as well as there, in wars of terror. The stories that could not be told in film or wallpaper find expression through hip-hop, as a medium where witness and documentary truth-telling coexist with an aesthetics of verbal and visual play, and an erotics of sexualisation and stylised excess. Through the performativity of hip-hop, with its primary reliance on technologies of breath, voice and body, the guerrilla stories of a distant war zone merge with an insurgent metropolitan tactics of survival. Yet, as Jayna Brown indispensably points out, transposed in space and time from the revolutionary politics of her father's generation, the music registers:

> a gap between the utopian desires around which the wars began, and what the wars are now, a gap filled with ambivalence... Filled with gunfire, bombs, and random explosions of electrified sound, her music may defiantly claim the right to fight, but it also recognizes that war cultures are what have formed out of many of the African and Asian revolutionary movements of the 1970s. (2010, 139)

This ambivalence is apparent even in the early 'Sun Showers' (2003), filmed on location in South India, which simulates the scene of a jungle guerrilla camp, with its ranks of women soldiers recalling the LTTE's famed female cadres, *Suthanthira Paravihal* (Birds of Freedom). In the video, the lines of armed women march one way, while M.I.A. swaggers in the opposite direction, sweetly singing.

Together with the publicity generated by M.IA.'s family anecdotes following the release of *Arular*, her repeated use of tiger motifs and images, such as those in 'Sun Showers', inevitably led to her being linked

DOI: 10.1057/9781137444646.0008

with the LTTE (Christgau 2005; Getler 2009). Also provocative were her references to being 'a guerrilla' which played on the tensions between popular and literal meanings of the term: between hip-hop as a guerrilla art form, the guerrilla status of racial outsiders in the western metropolis, and the bloody guerrilla war being waged in Lanka.

The popularity of M.I.A.'s early singles, and indeed, her emergence as an artist, coincided with a period when the Lankan war had achieved a new level of global visibility outside diaspora communities, re-inflected by the rhetoric of the war on terror. Some critics accused M.I.A. of exploiting the publicity this generated, while others, the Lankan government among them, accused her of being an apologist of the LTTE (Sarvananthan 2009). Still others saw her as 'simplistic' and unknowing in her references to Tamil oppression (Kadirgamar, quoted in Hirschberg 2010). The instant association of Tamil militancy with the LTTE is perhaps inevitable, given that by the 1990s, the LTTE had ruthlessly eliminated all its rivals for leadership, including EROS, the movement that Arular helped found. D'Lo noted that her family's allegiances had shifted in the course of the decade: her father moved from 'being a full-fledged Tiger supporter' in the aftermath of the 1983 pogroms, to retracting his support for them after Rajiv Gandhi's assassination by Dhanu, a female fighter of the LTTE, in 1991. In her later interviews, M.I.A. is careful to distinguish between Tamil people and the LTTE: 'From day one, what I've been saying is that I'm here for the people, talking about the citizens, not the Tigers. I don't know the Tigers, I don't know what they do…It's about the Tamil people, because I only know it from that experience' (Sawyer 2010).

Despite these disclaimers, Brown notes, 'within the music's ambivalence and ambiguity' there still 'lingers a romanticized notion of violence' (2010, 139), just as a desperate investment in the heroic aura of the LTTE continues to retain a place among some diasporic Tamils. As M.I.A.'s own earlier autobiographical anecdotes reveal, affective investments in the symbols and rhetoric of Eelam and Tamil militancy are a complex affair for many young Tamils, whose cultural and emotional landscape was shaped, perhaps unconsciously at times, but often more directly, by the politics of the post-1983 diaspora and its support for a separate homeland, Tamil Eelam.

As the exemplar of Black nationalism amply demonstrates, hip-hop is a medium in which nationalism's ambiguities, its liberating *and* destructive energies, can be simultaneously articulated, where violence

DOI: 10.1057/9781137444646.0008

in its multiple ramifications may be explored, celebrated and disowned, through its characteristic expressive modes of excess and oppositionality. Hip-hop is also a medium that enables the juxtaposition of the banal and the unspeakable that make up the disjunctive everyday of refugee and migrant lives: the realities of survival in strange and hostile new environments, the underground circulation of news from 'home', the bizarre-but-true rumours, fears and suspicions, and the tortuous local conflicts that characterise life in fringe communities. In this uncertain, submerged and diasporic multiverse, contradictory and competing understandings of the Tigers, as both heroic and murderous, protectors and predators, might easily coexist.

The hip-hop historian Jeff Chang beautifully describes the relationship between M.I.A.'s music, war, and diasporic audiences:

> On *Arular*, she broadcast the sound of those with one foot in the First World door, the other in a Fourth World gutter…Her spray-can and stencil art featured images of young gunmen flashing peace signs or bereted, barekneed Third World female soldiers marching en masse. But those images—like *Arular*'s words and sounds—weren't just about war, sex and revolution; *they were about what it means to consume those ideas.* Against a media flow that suppresses the ugliness of reality and fixes beauty to consumption, M.I.A. forces a conversation about how the majority live. She closes the distance between 'here' and everywhere else. (Chang 2007, my emphasis)

As attempts to 'force a conversation' about the violent disjunctions *and* the indissociable interconnections that simultaneously define the relationship between 'here and everywhere else', M.I.A.'s music speaks to diasporic subjects in direct and specific ways. Its shifting affective identifications and uncertain and ambivalent political allegiances reflect not only the consumption of *ideas* about war and revolution, but also the representations through which these take hold: mediatised fragments, migrant mythologies, and fragments of memory combine with the subterranean histories wordlessly transmitted in diasporic families and communities.

Living political

While *Arular*, the album named for M.I.A.'s father, speaks to diasporic generations who grew up consuming the images from a war that was both intimately experienced and spatially distant, M.I.A.'s second album,

DOI: 10.1057/9781137444646.0008

Kala (2007) named for her mother, is shaped by the post-9/11 years that brought third world terror and suicide bombing to the heart of metropolitan New York and London. Although the album was originally planned as a collaboration between M.I.A. and US hip-hop artists, M.I.A.'s application for a working visa in the post-9/11 United States was delayed for two years, presumably because of suspicions that she was linked to the LTTE. The Lankan government had been quick to proclaim its commonalities with the United States and its allies in these years, claiming the mantle of a sovereign state beset by terrorists; at the same time, moves to target violent Islamists and transnational terror networks had an impact on the LTTE abroad, and contributed to the waning of its grip on Tamil diaspora communities.

Unable to move to New York as planned, M.I.A. travelled to Liberia, India, Angola, Aboriginal Australia, Trinidad and Jamaica. While racial profiling and Islamophobia were rife in London in the years before and after the 7/7 bombings, M.I.A.'s music comes face to face with third world war zones, slums and border towns, where the sense of being under attack is nothing new. In these places, she comments, 'I had to morph…from being lyrically political into just living political'. The voice in *Kala* is edgy, grating, often unintelligible and non-verbal, punctuated by shrieks, explosions and gunshots. Yet it is also rhythmic, infectious, erotic, joyous. Sasha Frere-Jones wrote in the *New Yorker*: 'It's a voice from a place where kids throw rocks at tanks, where people pull down walls with their bare hands. It could be the sound of a carnival, or a riot' (2012).

This lived insurgent political embodied in *Kala* is 'a voice from a place where kids not only throw rocks at tanks', but carry Kalashnikovs, from Colombo to Congo:

> The music on this album registers the profound ethical ambiguity accompanying modern wars. It does not have the self-righteousness of justified violence, but it also does not escape that ethos. It allows in the voice of child soldiers, with their Kalashnikov lifestyles. It gestures to deeper dystopias [of child soldiers and] paramilitaries with the use of methamphetamines and gunpowder, [who] grow to enjoy the bonding rituals of violence. But within the music's ambivalence and ambiguity lingers a romanticized notion of violence. (Brown 2010, 139)

In its constitutive ambiguities, Brown points out, M.I.A.'s music is dance music, of the sort that compulsively engages and enthrals. 'The shrieks and clonks and horns are the anarchic sounds of turbulent movement and irrepressible play' (ibid.). As sounds from a place where people try

DOI: 10.1057/9781137444646.0008

to 'pull down walls with their bare hands', the music recalls Audre Lorde's meditation on the force of the erotic, harnessed through music, dance and other forms of creativity. For Lorde, as an empowered, specifically feminist, creative, embodied force, the erotic fuels resistance, defiance and joy in the face of repression and violence. 'In touch with the erotic', Lorde writes, 'I become less willing to accept powerlessness or other supplied states of being... such as resignation, despair, self-effacement, depression, self-denial' (1984, 56). The power of this music and movement, 'is not generated out of forgetfulness or nostalgia'. It is, rather the 'pulse of the utopian *energeia*' (Brown 2010, 139–40).

By all media necessary

The irrepressible energeia of M.I.A.'s music is inseparable from the technological conditions of its emergence: a landscape of pre-recorded samples, computer-generated mixes, file-sharing and the internet (Brown 2010, 139). In her analysis of the production of M.I.A.'s music, Meenakshi Durham turns to Chela Sandoval's groundbreaking articulation of a 'methodology of the oppressed' to understand M.I.A.'s ability to deploy 'do-it-yourself technologies' and alternative distribution networks, bypassing the music industry's corporate processes (Durham 2009).

I would extend Durham's analysis to argue that M.I.A.'s adoption of the methodology of the oppressed goes beyond production and distribution, offering a blueprint for the entirety of her practice of an embodied diasporic hip-hop poetics. 'The methodology of the oppressed', Sandoval writes, 'is formulated and taught out of the shock of displacement, trauma, violence and resistance'. Its practitioners are those who

> recogniz[e] their places and bodies as narrativized by and through the social body, and who are thus self-consciously committed to unprecedented forms of language, to remaking their own kinds of social position utilizing all media at their disposal—whether it is narrative as weapon, riot as speech, looting as revolution. (2000, 77–8)

Kala, with its kaleidoscopic mobilisation of visual, sonic and kinetic elements is an attempt at just such an unprecedented language.

Sandoval identifies the methodology of the oppressed with a 'differential consciousness' associated with the work of US third world feminists operating from diasporic or 'third space' locations, such as Audre Lorde's

DOI: 10.1057/9781137444646.0008

figure of the 'Sister Outsider' or Gloria Anzaldua's new *mestiza* (ibid., 66). Drawing from the era's various typologies of counterdiscourse—equal-rights (liberal-integrationist), revolutionary, supremacist (cultural-nationalist), separatist—differential consciousness is, above all, the ability to 'weave between and among' oppositional ideologies and positions, deploying them as '*tactics* for intervening in and transforming social relations':

> The differential represents the variant; its presence emerges out of correlations, intensities, junctures, crises. Yet the differential depends on a form of agency that is self-consciously mobilized in order to enlist and secure influence; the differential is thus performative. (ibid., 61)

The differential manoeuvring of the methodology of the oppressed produces 'a sleight of consciousness that activates a new space: a cyberspace, where...oppositional praxis can begin' (ibid., 63). It is in this cyberspace that I locate M.I.A.'s body of work, as it instantiates the methodology of the oppressed, deploying 'narrative as weapon', to produce 'unprecedented forms of language', using 'all media at [her] disposal'.

Born Free

In April 2010, the music and accompanying video of 'Born Free', a track from M.I.A.'s then-unreleased album, *Maya* (2011), was leaked on-line and then later released via her official website. The video—more precisely, a 9-minute short-film directed by Romain Gavras—caused instant controversy. It represented, in exacting, graphic detail, the round-up and wholesale slaughter of a seemingly random group of people in a dawn raid by masked SWAT troops. Every aspect of the raid and mass killing recalls news reports of some distant war zone—with the exception of one small but crucial detail: the targets, like the soldiers, are all pale-skinned. And only one other small characteristic differentiates the killers from killed: the victims all have red hair. This, then, is a war zone set in an imagined first world, where those being slaughtered in cold blood are *us*, not them.

The dawn raid, the round-up of the targets, the nightmare quality of their transport through urban streets, and their brutal massacre in a minefield into which they are forced at gunpoint, are all rendered in unsparing detail, accompanied by a punishing sound-track of sirens,

DOI: 10.1057/9781137444646.0008

heavy machinery, electronics, explosions and M.I.A.'s shrieking, discordant, mostly unintelligible sounds. The video sparked an outcry, presumably because of its collapsing of the distance between 'here' and 'everywhere else' to bring home the unthinkable. One scene in particular, the image of an angelic, freckle-faced, red-haired boy shot dead at close range, provoked outrage among viewers, generating a petition by US schoolchildren. It was removed from YouTube before being restored on restricted view for audiences over 18.

M.I.A.'s comment on the ban was simple: 'It's just fake blood and ketchup and people are more offended by that than the execution videos' that were also on YouTube (Sawyer 2010). The execution videos she refers to, subsequently authenticated by the UN, record the systematic shooting of a group of naked, unarmed, blindfolded men by Lankan government troops (see Preface). M.I.A.'s response to the ban on 'Born Free' called attention to the dissociations and double standards that enable viewers to be repulsed and offended by the staged death of a red-haired, white-skinned child, and yet to countenance the real-life killings of other innocent (non-white) children, with the tacit complicity, as in Lanka, or active involvement, as in Iraq or Palestine, of western governments. In the weeks and months after the war ended, recordings on mobile phones documented many such killings on the shores of Mullivaikkal and elsewhere. Underscoring that the Lankan case was only one instance of a wider phenomenon, Gavras questioned, 'How can you be shocked by the M.I.A. video and not shocked when Israel bombs Gaza for days and days… [a few months previously in the Operation Cast Lead of 2008]. Really crazy stuff where people actually die, real things?' (Cochrane 2010)

In the context of the totality of M.I.A.'s cultural production, I read 'Born Free' as a work that mobilises all media at her disposal to challenge dissociations and asymmetries of spectatorship that have become increasingly intolerable, in the context of wars of terror in Lanka and elsewhere:

> I was that kid on the telly when people were watching Sri Lanka on the news. For 10 years I lived like that, and I'm totally proud of it. I'm not about taking sides. I'm simply representing the refugee, a faceless thing, and I will always speak to that… Those are the roots, and I don't think they'll ever beat that out of me. My point is: people are investing millions of [dollars] in ammunition to bomb other people around the world, [and as long as they are] there will always be someone coming up from those places talking about it, because

DOI: 10.1057/9781137444646.0008

we've got the right. If they don't fill my head up with those images, then I won't be talking about it, and if they don't like it, they should stop first. (Orlov 2005)

Understood not as transparent documents, but complex media, M.I.A.'s hip-hop poetics bring to the surface the nightmare images and subterranean histories of war, massacre and displacement. Beyond the closed circle of diaspora groups, they bear witness, in the global sphere, to the unspeakable violence of small, hidden wars, and to the hidden stories of that 'faceless thing', the refugee.

DOI: 10.1057/9781137444646.0008

3
White Shores of Longing: Castaway Stories and Nation Dramas

Abstract: *Chapter 3 discusses scattered dramas of arrival and the citizenship of Tamil refugees in Australia and London. At the centre of the chapter is a play,* Theatre of Migration, *directed by the influential Tamil-Australian dramatist Ernest Thalayasingham MacIntyre.*

Keywords: castaway; citizenship tests; impossible subjects; *Lucky Miles*; *Theatre of Migration*

Perera, Suvendrini. *Survival Media: The Politics and Poetics of Mobility and the War in Sri Lanka.* New York: Palgrave Macmillan, 2016. DOI: 10.1057/9781137444646.0009.

DOI: 10.1057/9781137444646.0009

A true story threads this chapter together, the story of an arrival—of sorts. It concerns the experience of a group of Tamil asylum seekers from Lanka seeking to escape the war at home. Dropped off by boat off the coast of Coral Bay, in remote Western Australia, they were discovered some days later, in several small groups, wandering in the bush. As was recounted, with some hilarity, in the national media, the arrivals, all men, had come ashore dressed in their best suits to be ready for prospective job interviews, but had their trouser legs rolled up and shoes slung across their shoulders to wade through the waves. When one group came across a passing telephone linesman, they asked him for directions to the bus. The linesman stopped to fill their near-empty cans with water—then left to telephone the police. His commentary, as reported in the *Sydney Morning Herald* (2001), is deadpan:

> They were all very polite, and each of them shook my hand and told me they were Sri Lankan...You could tell that they didn't fit in, and they looked like they were dressed in their Sunday best...they were really weak when they shook my hand...Once we had managed to make sense of each other's English I told them there was a bus coming to pick them up, the cops' bus.

This scene on a beach is emblematic of a thousand others. Refugees from war, political persecution or impoverishment flee the source of their suffering dressed in their finest, ready to present their best face to their new home. They stand at the hostile and alien threshold of this destination, inappropriate, vulnerable figures, diminished by the ominous forces that loom over them. Faint with starvation and thirst, they hold out their weak hands in introduction, repeat their unintelligible names, and the name of that place to which they can never return. Their unspoken solicitation, with its silent messages of courtesy, respect and anticipatory hospitality, is met with what Joseph Pugliese has aptly described as the 'serviceable brutality' (2005, 304) of the grudging host, one who stops to fill their canteens with water before consigning them to the space of the detention camp, the holding place for the uncitizen at the limits of the nation. Welcome to Australia.

This story of the aborted arrival at Coral Bay is glossed by a scene in the play *Rasanayagam's Last Riot*, by the Tamil-Australian playwright, Ernest Thalayasingham MacIntyre. *Rasanayagam's Last Riot*, a powerful, emotionally fraught and politically complex work about Black July, ends with the murder of Rasanayagam on the streets of Colombo as the police stand by, and the departure of his friends, Sita and Philip, for Australia.

DOI: 10.1057/9781137444646.0009

In transit at an airport lounge in Singapore, they hear a report on TV about a massacre the LTTE has carried out against innocent Sinhala villagers, and a statement made by then Australian Foreign Minister Bill Hayden (later Governor-General) that this act removes 'the moral edge that the Tamils has been claiming for themselves'. Sita responds, 'It's good to know that the Australian Foreign Minister is interested in the moral edge, must be a nice place we are going to' (MacIntyre 1990, 50).

Nearly three decades later, the 'moral edge' of Australian political life is located precisely on the fault lines of refugee policy. The moral edge casually reveals itself in the serviceable brutality of the linesman who assures the Coral Bay refugees that 'there is a bus coming to meet them' before promptly summoning 'the cops' bus'. The derisive reporting of this incident in the national media underscores the symbolic and physical violence embedded in the failure/refusal of the citizen to recognise either legal or ethical responsibilities of care and hospitality towards the refugee cast away on its shores. This refusal/betrayal of the ethic of hospitality at the threshold nation reaffirms the place of the citizen, as it locates the refugee/castaway as a pivotal figure in contemporary enactments of citizenship.

This is a chapter about thresholds, literal and symbolic, about the frontiers of citizenship in disparate scenes, places and modes of representation. In *Impossible Subjects*, Mae Ngai argues that 'the central problem in U.S. immigration policy in the twentieth century' was the undocumented alien, as 'a person who cannot be and a problem that cannot be solved', inhabiting an in-between space in which 'citizenship's threshold and its character are deeply interwoven'. These impossible subjects—not-quite citizens—provide the invisible labour on which the economic viability of the US depends, even as its political and cultural identity requires their exclusion (2004, 3–6). At the beginning of the twenty-first century, in Australia, the US and the UK, the refugee and the asylum seeker are merged with figures of the 'economic migrant', the 'illegal' and the unassimilable as paradigmatic noncitizens, those whose presence on the frontier delimits and defines national space and licenses the political and economic asymmetries that prevail within (Stratton 2009). The asylum seeker coheres this territorialised national body and, in a parallel move, is located as the pivotal figure in contemporary enactments of citizenship.

In using the term enactment I seek to focus on the interrelations between the legal-political and the sociocultural aspects of citizenship: that is, citizenship as a category constituted by the legislative acts of the

DOI: 10.1057/9781137444646.0009

state, as well as one that is, as May Joseph puts it, enacted in the 'sphere of metaphoric, literal, and performed possibilities available in the everyday through which communities and individuals access (successfully or not) the experience of citizenship' (1999, 3). The extent to which citizenship can be accessed, and bodies positioned as legitimate or illegitimate occupants of civic space, depends on their ability to perform citizenship, through acts of speech, demeanour, gesture, consumption and display.

Embedded in the term enactment, at the same time, are what Lisa Lowe describes as acts of 'labor, resistance, memory and survival' in which 'unrepresentative histories of situated embodiment... contradict the abstract form of citizenship' enshrined in law (1996, 9; 7). As embodied practices, enactments of citizenship contradict and complicate the body of the state's legislative acts. They re-present the embodied histories of that which, at different stages of the national story, is placed outside the law, and as such, they fissure law's claims to a unified, abstract, disembodied and transcendent relation to the citizen. Bodies once disallowed expose the law's partial and contingent nature—although they may serve simultaneously to recuperate or rehabilitate this fractured body through teleologies of national inclusion or reconciliation.

'Close scrutiny of the ways in which citizenship is actually embodied by the state', Joseph writes,

> discloses a scenario filled with the anxious enactments of citizens as actors. The stock characters in this scenario include authentic citizens; inauthentic minorities; noncitizens... [and] emergent political subjects... an imagined geography of performed sites through which notions of the citizen as a 'legal' and 'cultural' subject emerge in tandem with the invention [or reproduction] of statehood. (1999, 5)

In what follows, I track such nervous enactments of embodied citizenship at the intersection of law, land (as territorialised geo-body) and nation, in the UK, Sri Lanka and Australia, the sites of different, but deeply entwined, dramas of citizenship that attempt to solve the question of the nation's impossible subjects.

Castaway stories

It is only in the first frames of its opening sequence that Michael James Rowland's 2007 Australian film about boat refugees, *Lucky Miles*, evokes

DOI: 10.1057/9781137444646.0009

the refulgent lyricism of the 1939 love poem by W.H. Auden that, presumably, inspired its title:

> Warm are the still and lucky miles,
> White shores of longing stretch away
> A light of recognition fills
> The whole great day, and bright
> The tiny world of lovers' arms.

At first, the connection between poem and film might appear slight, even fanciful. But this is a poem of yearning and arrival, exile and homecoming. Its imagined scene of arrival is a beach: 'Restored! Returned! The lost are borne/ On seas of shipwreck home at last' (Auden 1976).

This organising conceit, one that casts the body of the loved one as a dreaming, secret shore which the lover strives to reach, tossed by tempestuous currents amidst 'seas of shipwreck', is premised on an enduring trope of colonial discourse. In Auden's love poem, two distinct but connected figures, the literary construct of castaway, and its silent historical shadow, the refugee, brush against each other, though they do not quite meet. Earlier that year, declaring European civilisation 'done for', Auden and his friend Christopher Isherwood had begun a self-imposed exile from the UK that would last for the greater part of their lives (Osborne 1980, 185–9). In this context, the poem's coastline of desire, the 'white shores of longing' towards which it strives, appears, in the terms of a famous line from Donne's Elegy XIX, as a mapping of Auden's Newfoundland, the United States, on to the America of a lover's waiting body.

At the same time, the departure of Auden and Isherwood, prominent anti-fascist intellectuals, connects to a far more desperate exodus from Europe. In 1935, Auden went through a ceremony of marriage with Erika Mann, daughter of the novelist Thomas Mann, when she was threatened with the loss of her German citizenship as 'a public enemy of the Third Reich'. He urged other gay men to make similar marriages—'After all, what are buggers for?' (Osborne 1980, 109; 119). 'Refugee Blues', the opening poem of the sequence '10 Songs' in which 'Warm are the still and lucky miles' appears as number three, is an explicit comment on the predicament of refugees from Nazi Germany:

> Thought I heard the thunder rumbling in the sky;
> It was Hitler over Europe, saying, 'They must die'.

(W.H. Auden, 'Refugee Blues' [1976])[1]

DOI: 10.1057/9781137444646.0009

Much as Auden's 'Stop all the clocks' found new life as an elegy for the
AIDS era after being featured in the film *Four Weddings and a Funeral*,
since the early 2000s 'Refugee Blues' has circulated on the Internet as a
comment on the plight of asylum seekers brought to a standstill at the
border. 'Refugee Blues' evokes an all too familiar scene of recent years:
people in rickety, overcrowded boats, held at bay by invisible lines in
the sea. Packed on unseaworthy craft, hidden in shipping containers
or unprotected in their own fragile 'boat of one skin', contemporary
castaways wash up on the white shores of Europe, North America and
Australia (Hulme 2005, 197; Pugliese 2006). It is significant that to tell
the story of these other castaways, Auden turns to the blues, the cultural
expression of Afro-American forced removal and dispersal. The canoni-
cal literary trope of the castaway referenced in 'Warm are the still and
lucky miles' cannot encompass their stories, even as they constitute its
hidden conditions of possibility. The stanzas of 'Refugee Blues' echo, like
a type of historical chorus, the fraught and violent mobilities of refugee
bodies in ensuing decades, and the relations of fear, anxiety and hatred
they generate, as well as the legislative prohibitions and exclusions
designed to stop them in their tracks.

In his powerful essay, 'Cast Away', Peter Hulme has pointed out
the disjunction that prevails between the contemporary castaways
of globalisation and late capitalism and the prototypical castaway of
colonial discourse—the solitary, usually white and male, individualist
marooned on a desert shore to begin over again the labour of reproduc-
ing his world. Such Crusoe myths remain alive today in the manufac-
tured deprivations of *Survivor* and similar 'reality television' programs
set on ever more exoticised faraway coasts. What remains unspoken,
unspeakable, in these compulsive re-enactments of the castaway plot are
the collective stories of empire's historical and present-day refugees, of
whole peoples cast away in the name of progress, casually removed from
their homelands to lives in the brutal enclosure of a camp or exiled to
foreign shores. Hulme reminds that 'Although the trope of the castaway
is usually limited to individuals or small groups, and almost exclusively
European or North American, the colonial period saw many indigenous
groups quite literally cast away' (2005, 194).

Hulme's essay is invaluable in drawing lines of connection between
colonial acts of mass casting away of colonised peoples and the contemporary stories of those who increasingly have no option but to become
castaways. Their stories constitute the underside of tourist brochures

DOI: 10.1057/9781137444646.0009

advertising escape packages to remote tropical islands or *Survivor*-type fantasies staged on deserted coasts. These are the *other*, invisibilised, quests for sea change: 'To an extent rarely equalled since Shakespeare invented the phrase, those in search of a sea change to their lives are setting themselves on dangerous courses across water—Cubans and Haitians toward Florida, Southeast Asians toward Australia, Africans and other Asians toward Europe' (ibid., 196). *The Tempest*, peopled almost entirely by castaways, as Hulme marks, is a point of origin for both types of sea change stories, and for the twin significations of the island as place of refuge. Prospero and Sycorax, the chief antagonists on the island, are both what might be described in today's terms as political refugees. While Prospero is restored to his home after a long exile, Sycorax's fate is eternal incarceration. From its first use in a song designed by Ariel to bamboozle Ferdinand into thinking his father, Alonso, is dead, the phrase *sea change* itself is invested with double meaning: 'the literal changes brought about by salt water, from drowning to preservation; and the transformations experienced by those who cross the sea' (Hulme 2004, 187).

At the end of *The Tempest*, Alonso is discovered to be alive, but to have been transformed by his immersion in salt water. The film *Lucky Miles*, too, I will argue, replicates this movement from tragedy to comedy, from the possibility of death by water to a more fortunate sea-change— transformation into the deserving Australian subject. This happy ending is achieved through a movement from the figure of the refugee to that of the castaway, a movement that involves a reaffirmation of the nation and its inclusivist teleologies, as well as the assumption of assigned roles within the citizenscape.

An empire blues

But before returning to the beach, a historical detour, via another threshold of arrival, the airport: it is Heathrow in September 2007. I am in the UK to speak at a conference in Brighton, Interrogating Terror. An incredulous Anglo-Australian woman stands behind me in the immigration queue. The scene has changed since she and I have last been here. The line that differentiated passport holders from, effectively, the white diaspora states (Canada, Australia, New Zealand) as against other former British colonies has disappeared. In place of the old queues that were markedly segregated by colour and race, we now face the stark

DOI: 10.1057/9781137444646.0009

alternatives: 'EU Passports' and 'Others'. My Anglo-Australian compatriot can't quite believe it. She goes to check with an immigration officer before returning to her companions and announcing disconsolately, 'Yes, we've got to stand here. We're the others, apparently'.

Her chagrin is, in one sense, entirely understandable. Australian citizenship, for most of its history, was coextensive with British citizenship. At federation, the new state of Australia chose not to establish a distinctive category of Australian citizenship, but rather exercised its newly acquired sovereignty through the prohibition of non-white migration and other forms of border control. Henry Reynolds argues that in the absence of substantive independence from Britain, the government of the newly federated Australia was able to 'assert its independence not by hauling down the Union Jack but by closely controlling who and what could enter the country through tariffs, immigration controls, customs and quarantine regulations. These restrictions, rigorously exercised, came to be the surrogate assertion of independence by an impaired nation state' (2007, 66). Border control over people and goods operated in tandem with the continued definition of citizenship in racial terms and through subjection to Britain. Brian Galligan and John Chesterman identify this 'deliberate eschewing of citizenship in favour of subjecthood' to Britain and the exclusion of 'non-white groups' as 'evidence of Australia's non-citizenship tradition' (1999, 76–7) revealing, crucially, that the constituent elements of Australian citizenship are exclusion of non-white subjects and the racial link to British ancestry.

The outburst from the woman in my immigration queue at Heathrow was perhaps provoked by her sense that this historical compact between Australian and British citizenship was being abandoned. I wished I could have offered her a copy of Arun Kundnani's *The End of Tolerance* by way of explanation. Kundnani tracks the progressive erasure of Britain's imperial entanglements in immigration policy since the Second World War: 'Those who had been made into colonial subjects as Britain expanded its imperial rule over multiple "races" were now to be excluded from the white nationality that Britain sought in a context of contracting sovereignty' (2007, 15). During the 1960s and 1970s, Britain sought to jettison its non-white Commonwealth subjects while retaining its links with white diaspora states such as Australia through the biologised concept of 'patriality'. Growing up in post-independence Lanka, I could have charted the workings of this policy in the narratives of my friends and neighbours seeking to emigrate a climate of oppressive Sinhala

DOI: 10.1057/9781137444646.0009

nationalism. Now, a white grandparent, once a skeleton in the cupboard, suddenly became the pivotal figure in many a family tree, as white 'patriality' became a lifeline to Australia or the UK.

From the 1960s to the 1990s, British immigration policy was sustained by two complementary strategies: the adoption of measures, such as the racist construct of 'patriality', to restrict immigration from former non-white colonies, and the upholding of an official policy of domestic multiculturalism that provided minimal recognition and rights to the non-white citizens already within its borders (Kundnani 2007). This uneasy policy of promoting multiculturalism within national limits as a trade-off for strict controls on non-white immigration at the border has since been supplanted by a re-emphasis on 'cohesion' and 'core values', with the effect of revalorising whiteness and affirming an implicitly racialised model of British citizenship. In the 1980s, anxieties over globalisation, EU membership, sovereignty and the out-of-control welfare state were collected around the figures of the non-white migrant and asylum seeker, who came to be cast as

> potent symbols for the loss of a nation-state that once 'belonged' to its people and afforded them certain privileges as citizens... [T]he icon of the asylum seeker not only came to stand in for new kinds of migrations that globalised capitalism had produced but also became a screen on to which [anxieties around the diminishing sovereignty of the nation-state] could be projected. (ibid., 65–6)

Kundnani locates the moment when these anxieties came to a head in 1985, at the point when the first group of asylum seekers who were neither white nor fleeing communism arrived in Britain. They were Tamils who had fled following the pogrom of 1983, the early refugees of the war. To prevent their entry, for the first time, Commonwealth citizens arriving in Britain were now required to have a visa: in effect this meant that they had to arrive illegally because travel to Colombo or to a third country to apply for a visa was an impossibility for most (ibid., 39). On arrival, they were promptly stigmatised as 'economic migrants', rather than 'genuine refugees', a response, Kundnani argues that was to 'set... the template for a campaign against asylum seekers that would escalate relentlessly over the next two decades' (ibid., 66). Its culmination in the UK was a new model of race relations put forward in the 2002 White Paper on citizenship, symbolically reconfiguring whiteness through democracy, core 'values' and cohesion (read: assimilability) in the context of the war on terror (ibid., 5).

DOI: 10.1057/9781137444646.0009

Under the new dispensation, although white subjects from the white diaspora states of the Coalition of the Willing might have to endure the brief indignity of standing in the wrong immigration queue, the racialised reconfiguration of citizenship under the rubric of shared values and culture ensured their continued entrée into the national family. For those placed outside the pale in terms of cohesion and core values, on the other hand, the immigration queue represented only the first of a series of tests, checkpoints and blockages that circumscribed entry to both legal and cultural citizenship. This marked differentiation is nowhere more clearly manifested than immediately after passing through the immigration queue at Heathrow. My Anglo-Australian compatriot might look forward to jumping into a taxi, or collapsing into the arms of waiting friends, after enduring her ordeal in the Others' queue at Heathrow. But postcolonial itineraries of displacement and impoverishment, colonial processes of racial abjection, and the global city's unceasing demand for flexible, low-wage, low-status labour converge in the bodies of the non-white women from former British colonies, particularly South Asian women from Pakistan and Bangladesh, who clean the floors and toilets of Heathrow. At the intersection of colonial economies of representation and the gendered and raced counter-geographies of globalisation, the bodies of women re-orientalised by the war on terror into targets of suspicion and pity, and cast as the bearers of an obdurate 'cultural difference', serve in their heightened visibility and tacitly agreed on imperceptibility as object lessons of the uncitizen for new arrivals into the UK.

Australia: a brief history in check points

What Kundnani identifies as a watershed in British immigration policy—the arrival of Tamil refugees from the war in Lanka—is a key moment in my own biography. The 1983 anti-Tamil pogroms, and the escalation of violence that followed, caused the dispersal of my extended family out of Lanka. For me, already a sojourner in the west, they put an end to any idea of return 'home'. The cleaners at Heathrow airport, then, embody complex injunctions and reminders for me. Yet, I must not forget either that my escape from the worst effects of the war in Lanka were purchased by entry into a different theatre of colonisation, and mobilisation into another national war—the war in Australia.

DOI: 10.1057/9781137444646.0009

In the Australian state, founded on the denied sovereignty of Aboriginal and Islander people, the categories of white, non-white and black, of *native*, *alien* and *citizen* were from its inception constituted through interlocking inscriptions of alterity and sameness, by the hierarchies of colonial raciology and its performed differentiations and discriminations. The decision in 2006 to introduce a citizenship test through amendments to the 1948 citizenship act was both an extension and a reworking of what Galligan and Chesterman characterise as 'Australia's non-citizenship tradition', a tradition founded on the exclusion of any 'aboriginal [sic] native of Australia, Asia, Africa, or the Islands of the Pacific' (1999, 73–4). Neoliberal ideologies, an aggressive new program of assimilation, and the push for national security were the driving forces of the 2006 amendments. For Indigenous peoples these forces culminated in a military intervention into Aboriginal-run communities, positioned as internal failed states along the lines of those in the Pacific and the Middle East (Perera 2007). For migrants, the test instituted under the amended citizenship act recalls the infamous dictation test under the White Australia Policy (Reynolds 2007, 67), while replicating moves by Australia's senior partners in the Coalition of the Willing and the successive border protection acts adopted since 2001. As a nodal point for a number of immigration and assimilation policies, the test draws attention to a new space at the threshold of citizenship. Like the beach and the coastline, this symbolic threshold space at the frontier of citizenship is one that implicitly, and at times explicitly, references the figure of the asylum seeker.

The citizenship test as a new borderline, or checkpoint, targets the foreigner at the gates, making visible a new category of uncitizen, or infra-citizen, at the threshold of citizenship. Together with a constellation of other formal and informal practices, the test is a technology that subjects the aspiring citizen to a gaze that scrutinises, disciplines and separates. The proliferation of a number of lampoons and mock enactments of the citizenship test suggests a clear understanding of its function as performance, a script that the aspiring citizen must be able to deliver, more or less convincingly, with the aid of appropriate actions and props, as in Tim Brunero's lampooning of the citizenship test on the ABC's *Chaser* comedy show (Brunero 2007). As the test imposes a mode of performance on the infra-citizen, it is also a staging of 'national values', a set piece directed at the privileged subjects of the nation. As it recognises and reaffirms the histories and symbols of these privileged national subjects, the citizenship test is a nod to insider knowledge.

DOI: 10.1057/9781137444646.0009

On Australian television, commercials promoting the aims of the citizenship test replaced earlier advertisements that urged migrants to take up citizenship. Prior to the war on terror, dominant representations cast the achievement of citizenship as the culmination of the migrant narrative. The naturalisation or citizenship ceremony was the ultimate staging of arrival, the logical *telos* of the narrative of migration, although the closure it promised remained unachievable for differently raced and gendered bodies. The spectacle of migrants and refugees assuming national status, or becoming 'naturalised', affirms the ideal of a consensual liberal citizenship that allows existing citizens to 'reenact liberalism's fictive foundation in individual acts of uncoerced consent' (Bonnie Honing, quoted in Ngai 2003, 5). The shift from the citizenship ceremony as a staging of arrival and a liberal validation of choice, to a form of certification and a technology for separating out the unworthy and the suspect, re-signifies citizenship and makes it visible anew as a site where the limits of the national are enforced. A 2007 speech given by the Minister for Immigration and Citizenship, for example, specified that 'migrants who fail to show willingness to integrate into Australian society will be denied a permanent visa and face being sent back to their home country'. Moreover, it stipulated that 'specially trained officers will evaluate migrants' attitudes towards learning English and integrating when assessing their applications for permanent residency' (*The Australian* 2007). The spotlight cast on the threshold or frontier of citizenship re-enacts the literal policing of borders that has been at the forefront of Australian politics since, at least, the arrival of the *Tampa* in 2001, enacting the border policing of Australian citizenship as a search for the enemy within.

The *Theatre of Migration*

Theatre of Migration, a community production by diasporic Lankans in Sydney, premiered at Macquarie University's Lighthouse Theatre on the eve of the 2001 general election, in what came to be thought of as the *Tampa* election. The *Tampa* incident signified a watershed in contemporary Australia, when a Norwegian merchant ship, which had picked up asylum seekers in distress at sea, was refused permission to land. After a long standoff, the ship was stormed by SAS forces and the Iranian, Lankan and Afghan castaways aboard taken to offshore Pacific

DOI: 10.1057/9781137444646.0009

detention camps. The *Tampa* initiated the militarisation of refugee policy, with the navy now routinely deployed to intercept asylum boats. On the morning of the play, the cast awoke to the news that two women asylum seekers from Iraq, Fatima Husseini and Nurjan Husseini, had drowned when a fire broke out after the navy attempted to turn away their damaged boat from Australian waters. The women were the first known casualties directly attributable to new 'border protection' legislation, but their deaths followed the drowning of over 350 asylum seekers a fortnight earlier in the sinking of a mysterious Suspected Illegal Entry Vessel (SIEV), later known as SIEV X, in circumstances that remain to be accounted for (Perera 2006).

These were weeks of unprecedented tension as 'border protection' legislation was rammed through parliament, and public feeling against asylum seekers whipped into a frenzy following the 9/11 attacks. The border protection legislation had the effect of consolidating homeland and citizenship as raced and gendered categories, and placing under suspicion diasporic groups located at the fringes of a nation now reconfigured as a 'homeland' under siege. And as in the US, in this most attentive of its junior partners in the war on terror, communities and individuals re-orientalised and re-racialised as Muslim, Middle Eastern or South Asian, were put on notice to perform their allegiance in the absolutist terms demanded by President George W. Bush: 'Either you are with us, or you are with the terrorists' (2001).

News of the deaths added a sense of urgency to tensions already built up over the preceding weeks, as the cast engaged with the play's relation to charged debates on citizenship, refugees, terrorism, security and border protection. These debates re-inflected the investments that cast members brought to the production as a performance of cultural citizenship, as a 'dialectical process' of migrant self-making and self-representation in negotiation with the state (Ong 2003, 264). As a performance of cultural citizenship, *Theatre of Migration* encapsulated the contradictions and divides among diasporic Lankans, their disparate positions and formation through the forces of ethnonationalism and war.

The play, performed mostly in English, was put together by a cast of multiethnic, middle-class Lankan migrants—Burgher, Tamil, Sinhala, Muslim—led by Ernest Thalayasingham MacIntyre, a director with an established reputation in both Lanka and Australia. On one level, the play can be situated within a claim for political status undertaken by a recent migrant community: the staging of a claim for visibility and legitimation

DOI: 10.1057/9781137444646.0009

on the Australian scene (ibid., 266). At the same time, the making of the play inevitably brought to the surface cleavages and contradictions among a cast marked by a series of ethnic, religious, political and linguistic divides, and provided a forum for airing differences that would have been repressed in other social interactions between them. Unavoidably, internal conflicts over the meaning of terms like *terrorism, nation, citizen* and *rights* produced by the war 'at home'–in Lanka–also acquired new inflections in light of Australia's internal debates in the war on terror and the arrival of refugees.

A product of these split positions, *Theatre of Migration* emerged as a 'chaos of stories', a text cumulatively assembled, rather than authored (Perera 2001). As the play was put together, by argument, negotiation and adjudication, a process in which I participated both as dramaturg and contributor to the script, its dimensions expanded until it eventually reached back in time to include the period before the introduction of the White Australia Policy (that is, prior to the establishment of the Australian state), as well as forward to the present, to the refugee boats that seemed to be arriving almost daily. A defining moment for the direction that the play would take came when the decision was made to represent an event that occurred a few months earlier: the story of the Lankans dumped off the coast of Coral Bay, Western Australia. They were quickly consigned to the Detention Centre at Port Hedland—bleeding feet, inappropriate suits, strange accents and all—after asking the telephone linesman for directions to a bus stop.

Weaving their bloody trails on and off the set of *Theatre of Migration*, these starving, barefoot refugees invoked nameless figures from different times and places—unlawful non-citizens, illegals, disappeared and other 'impossible subjects' of the Australian state. Over 70 Lankan nationals were in detention in Australia at the time of the performance, incarcerated along with hundreds of more visible detainees from Iraq and Afghanistan in offshore camps on Nauru and Manus Island, Papua New Guinea. Beyond these were the shadows of scores of thousands more disappeared and 'internally displaced' as a result of 20 years of war and terror in Lanka. In the paired contexts of war, here and there, telling their stories triggered multi-layered frictions and fears among the ethnically mixed cast. Opposing allegiances in the war in Lanka mingled with domestic anxieties about the risks posed by 'illegals' and refugees to the aspirations of mostly professional, middle-class Lankan-Australians. Anxieties expressed by some of us over behaving like bad guests in our

DOI: 10.1057/9781137444646.0009

new home and straining the hospitality of our hosts were compounded by the real danger of appearing 'unAustralian' in dangerous times. These fears clearly indicated the limits that circumscribed both the play and the multicultural citizenship it aimed to perform.

Only a brilliant decision by the director allowed the production to proceed, not by resolving the incompatible political positions among the cast, but by staging them, literally, on a set divided into unequal parts: at one end, the comfortable, suburban domesticity of prosperous, apparently happily assimilated migrants; at the other, the bleak lines and harsh lights of a detention camp where the illegal, unruly and un-Australian were dispatched in the course of the action. Set apart from these two major divides was a small third space, suggesting a café or kitchen table, where a group of rambunctious old men drink arak, tell dirty jokes and reenact the history of Lankan migrants in Australia—a profane, irretrievably obtuse, anti-chorus. The action of the play shuttled between these spaces, from the airport lounge of legal arrival and the citizenship ceremony to inhospitable beaches on which refugees wander; from suburban *baila* parties to stories from behind the razor wire.

The temporal and spatial disjunctions of the play, its juxtapositions, asynchronous staging of heterogeneous lives, and interspersed song and dance numbers, projected the disparate stakes and positionalities among the cast. They enacted not only the absence of a unified diasporic community, but of any stable form of citizenship. At the same time, the division of the stage into these different kinds of space, 'inside' and 'outside', 'legal' and 'illegal', suggested not the absolute separation between the zones, but their contiguity, and the exchange between the categories of 'Australian' and 'un-Australian'. Against the razor wire and the detention camp, happy histories of arrival and assimilation faltered, while also frustrating neoliberal multiculturalism's demand for those stories described by Gayatri Spivak as 'bottom-line national origin validation' (Spivak 1996, 83). The un-Australian, illegal and impossible subjects of the play undermined the category of the assimilated Australian by making visible the contingencies and the complicities of citizenship in time and space, and revealing the limits of belonging. As a migrant act, *Theatre of Migration* performed the *other* Australian stories that not only disrupted the notion of a unified national identity but also refuted the fiction of a progressively inclusive nation. On this divided stage, the reconciliation of illegitimate migrant and refugee bodies into a national story was revealed as an impossibility.

DOI: 10.1057/9781137444646.0009

Fatal shores

Immediately following the opening titles of *Lucky Miles*, the viewer confronts a body struggling in the ocean, seemingly in the throes of drowning. Held in suspension under water, it is weighted down by awkward packages. Its hair streams alarmingly upwards. A froth of perfect bubbles issues from its mouth. The image is an immediate reminder of the fate of thousands of castaways in the years of the *Tampa* and SIEV X. In the next frame, these tragic expectations are confounded, as the body is lifted out of the sea, a helping hand under its head and back, evoking the gestures of immersion, baptism, rebirth. The rescued man laughs with delight as he emerges from the water. One by one, other bodies make landfall on the beach around him, allowing the viewer to anticipate, instead of the expected tragedy, a contemporary drama of redemption and sea-change.

But our expectations are once again confounded as the arrivals survey the stark coastline around them. Here is no welcoming landscape of arrival, unfolding like a lover's compliant body, but a harsh and barren shore. As the boat that conveyed them makes a hasty getaway with the assurance that there is a bus stop on the other side of the sand dunes, one of the arrivals protests, 'This does not look like a place where a bus stops'. Later we learn his name, Youssif, an engineer from Iraq. He is dressed, improbably, in a white suit; his trouser legs are rolled up and his shoes slung around his neck. Out of hearing, the sailor responds, sardonically, 'Welcome to Paradise!'

Lucky Miles is set entirely along the coastline of Western Australia. The main part of the action consists of the meanderings up and down this coastline by different groups searching for the road to Perth or to Broome. The new arrivals include asylum seekers from Iraq, chief among them Youssif, who obsessively rehearses the words of the UN Refugee Convention, reminding us of debates in the present over the alleged illegality of seeking asylum. There is also another group: young men from Cambodia. All their fathers are dead, presumably in the war, with one exception: Arun, who has come in search of his Anglo-Australian father who disappeared many years ago. Two Indonesian fishers moonlighting as 'people smugglers' separately wander the coastline, searching for Broome after their boat catches fire. It is a place they know well, as many Indonesian fishers are already imprisoned there for trespassing in Australian waters. In inept pursuit of them all are three Australian army

DOI: 10.1057/9781137444646.0009

reservists, two Aboriginal and one Anglo-Australian. In the wayward itineraries of these disparate parties, *Lucky Miles* stages a drama of contemporary citizenship that focuses attention on the beach, coastline and bush as entry points into Australia.

Stumbling in and doubling up on one another's footsteps, the reservists and the new arrivals at times appear to be equally at sea in the bush; like the radio command with whom they maintain sporadic contact, it seems they 'couldn't find their arse with both hands'. The presence of the two Aboriginal members who occasionally act as trackers lends the reservists a semblance of professionalism, while connecting the action to the 'lost in the bush' narratives of settler mythology—dramas in which Aboriginal guides play an ambiguous role as the insider-outsiders of a nation-in-the-making. The achievement of citizenship in the film is bound up with acts of fraternity and filiation in this landscape of coastline and bush that implicitly references the alien and hostile landscape experienced by early colonisers-settlers. Rather than a contemporary refugee drama, I read *Lucky Miles* as a yarn of multiethnic mateship, and an interracial family romance of sons and fathers. As Stratton points out, women are largely absent (2009). The all-male bush adventures of the characters mimic those of classic survivor-explorers as the new arrivals move from refugee histories into an increasingly familiar castaway plot.

Lucky Miles is one of the few Australian films featuring dialogue in Farsi, Bahasa Indonesia and Khmer, and where Indigenous, refugee and migrant actors play the key roles. Despite this, its narrative structure, tropes, landscape and characters are all part of a cinematic stock-in-trade, affirming an assimilationist injunction. The transition of the new arrivals from refugees to castaways culminates in an extended sequence reminiscent of classic explorer/survivor tropes, when three main characters make camp in an abandoned settler's hut and succeed, after days of effort, in repairing a rusty, damaged ute they find there. The moment when all three pile into the corroded, misshapen and broken ute and manage to steer it in unison marks their achievement of mateship, where previously they had quarrelled, cursed and abused one another. An unlikely metaphor for a ship of state, the ute sets the three castaways on the track to Australian citizenship. The bond between them is consolidated soon after, when Youssif and Ramelan disable one of the 'people smugglers' and then jointly give themselves up to the reservists.

At the climactic moment, Youssif walks forward towards these representatives of the state, formally invoking the words of the UN Refugee

DOI: 10.1057/9781137444646.0009

Convention. Unaccountably, the Anglo-Australian head of the unit stumbles at this point, conveniently leaving the Aboriginal reservist, Tom Collins, to receive Youssif's plea for asylum. He responds by declaring laconically, 'Yeah, okay.' In this gesture, *Lucky Miles* neatly sidesteps the problematic question of sovereignty. A momentary misstep stamps the grant of asylum by an Aboriginal man as an act that at once exceeds and falls short of official legitimacy. As if to underline this, Youssif reiterates his claim as the Anglo-Australian officer, once more in charge, radios back to base. This time he receives a hasty thumbs up in reply. The urgency of Youssif's claim is in sharp contrast to the casual responses it receives from the army officers. The taken-for-granted acknowledgement of Youssif's asylum claim enables forgetting, both of the earlier arrest of the Cambodian group at the pub, and of the unrelenting border protection regime in place at the time of the film's making and viewing. Instead, acts of reciprocal recognition confer inclusion in a nation whose historical burdens are increasingly bracketed as the plot progresses.

The scene with which I began—barefoot, starving Lankan asylum seekers asking directions to the bus—is enacted twice in *Lucky Miles*. The first time, it plays as tragedy when, shortly after their arrival, some of the Cambodians are hauled off by armed police after going into a pub to ask directions to the bus stop. Only one, Arun, manages to escape. In the final scene of the film, Arun, still stubbornly searching for the Australian father who abandoned him at birth, is driven to a bus stop by an improbable good Samaritan, an inscrutable kangaroo shooter. At last, waiting for a coach to Perth, under an advertisement for the Lucky Miles Bus Company, Arun collapses into sobs. His journey is over. The next scene finds him standing at the door of a middle-class house in a Perth suburb. It is shot, significantly, from within. An Anglo-Australian man opens the door with, 'What can I do for you, son?' In this moment, the fate of Arun's fellow castaways, the Cambodians hauled off at gunpoint on 'the cops' bus', is consigned to oblivion, and patriality provides the ultimate solution to question of the un-Australian subject.

(Im)possible subjects

In *Theatre of Migration*, the decision to represent the violence of Australian refugee policy in the end could not be separated from the state's long non-citizenship tradition and entailed a performance of its

DOI: 10.1057/9781137444646.0009

repressed histories of the non-citizen. As an immigrant act, the play's staging of unrepresentative lives invokes the impossible subjects of the nation, those limit-figures of citizenship. *Lucky Miles*, in contrast, is representative of the way refugee stories are enfolded and reframed within the citizenscape, through the incorporation of the main characters through fraternal and filial relationships. What must remain outside the film's frame are the spaces of the camp, and the hidden stories of what Joseph Pugliese describes as the 'theatres of cruelty' that are Australia's refugee prisons (2002).

And what of the unrepresentative subjects who leave their brief, indispensable, traces in these dramas of citizenship, and whose stories open up a momentary space at the threshold of nation, the space of the impossible subject, like that of the starving, barefoot asylum seekers of Coral Bay? Despite attempts to trace their stories, I can only glimpse them among the riots, hunger strikes and outbreaks of self-harm that occurred in Port Hedland in 2001–3, and imagine their consignment, among other recalcitrant inmates, to punitive detention in a camp within the camp. Media accounts and official reports, as well as writings by various refugees and advocates, document these events, as they do the forced deportation of asylum seekers to a number of places, including to Lanka, where they were subjected to abuse, violence and even death (CNN 2001; Edmund Rice Centre 2004, 2006). Against these stark events that block the passage of refugee bodies: a fleeting image or two, fragments of narrative that strain to account for the brief spaces where their lives touch ours, some bloodied footprints on a white beach of arrival.

Note

1   I am grateful to Edward Mendelson, literary executor and editor of W.H. Auden's works, for responding so promptly to my query about the original publication of 'Refugee Blues'.

DOI: 10.1057/9781137444646.0009

4

Accounting for Disposable Lives: Visibility, Atrocity and International Justice

Abstract: *Chapter 4 discusses questions of accountability for the tens of thousands of civilian lives lost in the last weeks of the war. Analysis centres on the satellite images recorded by various international agencies as forms of remote monitorship that represent, both metaphorically and materially, the hovering, telescopic oversight of international justice over this seemingly obscure war.*

Keywords: Lawfare, Mullivaikkal; LTTE; Nanthikadal; No Fire Zone; Operation Cast Lead; Operation Protective Edge; UN internal review

Perera, Suvendrini. *Survival Media: The Politics and Poetics of Mobility and the War in Sri Lanka.* New York: Palgrave Macmillan, 2016. DOI: 10.1057/9781137444646.0010.

This chapter deals with the final phase of the war in Lanka, the forms of violence it unleashed, and the lines of escape it opened up or rendered impassable. Beginning at the bitter end, the final defeat of the LTTE, it examines the successive geopolitical framings of the war, from an uncivil conflict on the margins of global attention to its recasting as an extended front of the war on terror and, finally, as a humanitarian catastrophe which reflects on of the international community and its institutions of justice. Against these shifting frames, the chapter tracks the dominant tropes and genres through which refugee and diaspora subjects are positioned in narratives of the war and its aftermath: as security threats to be contained and punished, as trauma subjects in need of rescue, and as artefacts of international shame. The discussion is shaped by questions of the limits and possibilities of an international order of justice and its economies of perception and visibility. The formulation The International Community (TIC) is employed throughout to signify the global institutions that are seen to administer and adjudicate matters of international justice. In March 2014, five years after the war's conclusion, the United Nations Human Rights Council (UNHRC) passed a resolution calling for an international inquiry into the conduct of the war in its final phase (OHCHR 2014). The same body had passed a contrary resolution just as the war ended, praising the Lankan state's victory (HRW 2009). The chapter follows the complicated stages between these two resolutions and their implications for the possibilities and limits of a justice administered by TIC.

The final stages of the war in Lanka, in May 2009, correspond with Israel's Operation Cast Lead in Gaza in late 2008 and early 2009, and TIC's responses to the two have been compared by prominent scholars such as Stephen Ratner (2012, 801). As punishing siege operations, with a terrible toll in civilian lives and environmental wreckage, the two share a number of features. In each of these siege situations, the states involved —Israel and Sri Lanka—represented themselves as extended fronts of the war on terror whose actions were vindicated by the ruthlessness of the terrorists they were facing. Their tactics were positioned as comparable to US counterinsurgency tactics in Iraq and Afghanistan. After the end of the war, counterinsurgency (COIN) theorists were quick to debate whether the 'Sri Lankan Model' could provide 'a different counterinsurgency template' for states such as Pakistan, Myanmar, the US and Israel (Beehner 2010). Like the contradictory resolutions on Sri Lanka, the United Nations'2009 Goldstone report on the Gaza death-siege has had a fraught and tortuous history in the UN.

DOI: 10.1057/9781137444646.0010

As Eyal Weizman and others point out, it is at the fringes and in 'an endless series of diffused border conflicts' that the body of international law is constantly reshaped and tested (2011, 91). Through my analysis of this war in a border zone and at the colonial limits, I seek to pose a set of questions about what forms of accountability are at play in processes of international justice that, even as they call for accountability for crimes against humanity, reproduce and reinscribe the very conditions that have rendered those lives already unlivable, disposable: bare life. At stake in these questions are the economies of visibility that underwrite international justice processes, the technologies of perception that render bodies visible or invisible and the forms of what Diana Taylor names 'percepticide' that structure the 'given-to-be-seen' and the 'given-to-be-invisible' of dirty wars at local and international scales (1997, 119). If the tropes of revelation and recognition are central to the credible functioning of an order of international justice, how are conditions of suffering and atrocity made visible within that order, and on what terms are accountabilities assumed and assigned for them? On what terms are subjects of the war's atrocities rendered available to be seen, and what are the structures and identities that enable their entry into global perceptibility? My analysis centres on satellite images recorded by various international agencies of the brutal final weeks of the war as forms of remote monitorship that represent, both metaphorically and materially, the hovering, telescopic oversight of international justice over this seemingly obscure war.

In plain sight

In May 2009, the thirty-year war between the Lankan state and the LTTE ended in the latter's utter military defeat. During the preceding months, as LTTE forces fell back before the Lankan army's advance, the government declared a sequence of 'Civilian Security Zones' (CSZs) and 'No Fire Zones'(NFZs) across the Vanni region in the north east. The stated aim of these zones was to protect displaced civilians caught up in the retreat, voluntarily and involuntarily mixed in with LTTE cadres fighting to hold on to their rapidly contracting territory. In practice, although the defeat of the LTTE was now all but inevitable, the entire population of the region was shelled and bombed through several temporary homes to these zones pinpointed by the state's own tactics to become 'the most bitterly contested' battleground of the entire war (UTHR [J] 2009, 17).

DOI: 10.1057/9781137444646.0010

This punitive approach to the local inhabitants positioned them as undifferentiated enemies and interlopers on the land, despite the state's rhetorical insistence that they were hapless 'hostages' in need of rescue from the LTTE.

Following a statement that the Lankan government would no longer guarantee their safety, TIC, in the form of the United Nations and NGOs, withdrew by painful stages, abandoning their both their local staff and the general population while assuring them of a speedy return (Malathy 2012, 143). This trope of retreat is a familiar one in global human rights and international justice narratives, and one to which I will return. As happened more publicly in Rwanda or Bosnia, this moment of retreat is often coupled with a repeated insistence on the helplessness or impotence of international institutions (Williams 2010, Hartman and Vulliamy 2015). The moment of formal withdrawal, I argue, constitutes a type of crux of visibility at which international justice publicly recognises itself in the very moment of its turning away, as it is called to an admission of its own failure. At the edges of its field of vision, in this very act of turning away, it sets the conditions of (in)visibility for the violence shortly to be unleashed, delimits the ground of its (our) knowledge of the human suffering that will ensue, and determines the measures by which accountability for that suffering will be assessed.

It is now indisputable from the evidence of classified diplomatic cables released by WikiLeaks and other sources that, despite its withdrawal from the scene, TIC remained well appraised of what was underway on a seemingly invisible and inaccessible patch of ground in the Vanni during the last months and weeks of the war in Lanka. Their awareness is evidenced in the nickname – The Cage – that international officials adopted for the region, even as a series of No Fire Zones were nominated by the state in a show of compliance with formal conventions for the protection of civilians in combat conditions (Weiss 2011).

Between January and May 2009, the civilians trapped in The Cage were hunted by the Lankan army on the one hand, and held, often forcibly, as cover by the LTTE forces on the other. They were already weak and ill, as systematic under-reporting of their numbers by the state meant that the carefully calculated Malthusian 'humanitarian minimum' of food aid dispensed to them by TIC was woefully inadequate (UTHR [J] 2009, 20; ICEP 2014; Hoole 2015). Incredibly, a UN internal review in 2012 states that 'The UN believed there to be about 350,000 [people in the Vanni region], but did most of its assistance planning on the basis of 200,000 beneficiaries', despite being aware that the 'LTTE may have taken up to 20% of assistance' for its forces (UN 2012, 55). The government put the figure of people in the region at only 70,000. Despite the starvation conditions in which these 'beneficiaries' were placed by the government, the LTTE and TIC, continuing attacks from shells and bombs from government forces compelled them to keep on the run. An official interviewed by the BBC journalist Francis Harrison reported:

> Ten displacements was the norm, and many arrived on foot. We would give them a hut. We kept finding people under mango trees; if they'd been hit by artillery in the night they just ran and jumped on the first tractor out...We started by handing out kits to construct shelters, and then we realised that they were building them and five days later, the same people were displacing. So it was pointless. We resorted to giving out three pieces of wood and a bit of tarpaulin so that they could carry it with them. (2012, Loc. 423)

Displacing and displacing yet again, carrying with them the pitiful means for the barest of shelters, three wooden sticks and a piece of tarp, feeding themselves on leaves boiled in sea water, hundreds of thousands of people made their way by weary stages in a frantic zig-zag across the no-exit of The Cage. Mired in shit and bloody corpses, as one witness described it (UTHR [J] 2009, 96), beset on every side by infernal sights, sounds and smells, they found themselves in the last days of the war, at the very edge of the third and final of the No Fire Zones, on a painfully narrow extremity of land at Mullivaikkal, hemmed in by opposing armies, with a lagoon on one side, the sea on the other.

Complementing TIC's rueful foreknowledge of the predicament of those ensnared in The Cage, the conflict zone was also silently monitored via what Allen Feldman terms the powerful 'securocractic' optical technologies that image famine-scapes, disaster-scapes, war-scapes and other cartographies of geopolitical risk (2006, 208). Such imaging technologies, despite their aspirations to omnipresence and omniscience, are marked by blind spots and zones of unseeing that screen, edit and structure objects, acts and relations within their field of vision, as they are also subject to mediation and framing by the national and supranational agencies which attempt to control their meanings.

From on high, the frantic displacing of people through the scrub and swamp-scape of The Cage was logged by Google Earth, and in more detail by the US Defense Department's National Geo-Spatial Intelligence Agency and the UN's Institute for Training and Research-Operational Satellite Applications Programme (UNITAR/UNOSAT). A

DOI: 10.1057/9781137444646.0010

2011 report confirms that UNOSAT was 'requested by the UN Resident Humanitarian Coordinator in Colombo, Sri Lanka to provide detailed imagery analysis during the final months of the civil war' (UNITAR 2011, 17). However, footage from these sources was only selectively released. At the time, UNITAR / UNOSAT received criticism for withholding the images from 19 April 2009, after first making them briefly available on line (Lee 2009). Even more disturbingly, the information gathered by the UNOSAT images was subsequently discredited by the UN's own resident coordinator in Colombo, who assured the government in writing that the visual evidence they presented of aerial bombardment was 'partial and provisional' (UN 2012 17). The government made good use of this letter to dismiss concerns about the shocking rate of civilian deaths inside its own declared No Fire Zone.

A crucial sequence of satellite images, only made publicly available after the war, documents the systematic destruction of the third and final of the No Fire Zones, recording the stage-by-stage deterioration of The Cage, as it is meticulously pounded into wasteland (*Groundviews* 2012). Under the impervious gaze of a sovereign technicity, the teeming dark green of this desperate enclave, thickly flecked with the luminescent white and blue of UN-issue tarpaulin, dulls and deadens, transforming into a corrugated topography of desert and dust. The beach sand, no longer white, dyes to an ominous rust; the brilliant blue-green of the surrounding waters turns clogged and murky. Against the scorched earth, a few tatters of dirty plastic are all that remain of any slight promise of human shelter this wrecked ground once held out.

The orbiting gaze makes no claim to interpret or adjudicate the changes it records in the soundless landscape. Its view remains, as Lisa Parks puts it in her essay on Srebrenica, that of super-vision, and of over-sight (2010, 264). The sudden disappearance of a cluster of blue and white flecks between one day and the next, after a period of what looks like cloud cover, may signify the use of scorching white phosphorus gas to screen advancing troops. The appearance of craters and piles of debris on ground where tents once stood, the reddening of a patch of sandy soil, are one kind of evidence of the use of weaponry (cluster munitions, multiple barrel rocket launchers, repeated aerial bombing) criminally at odds with the conditions at hand, where hundreds of thousands of civilians and wounded were closely packed in with a small number of enemy fighters (ICEP 2013). In the stated view of the Lankan government and its surrogates, on the other hand, the same pits and deep indentations

DOI: 10.1057/9781137444646.0010

on the coruscated earth of the NFZ signify bunkers and trenches dug for defensive purposes (Weiss 2011, 206).

What is indisputable is that each bright speck of plastic once represented a human cluster, a shelter built with three wooden sticks and a piece of tarp, a flimsy refuge for a family with children and elderly, or perhaps a makeshift medical tent for the wounded and ill. You can count the dots. After the fact, the UN did just that, averaging five people per dot, to estimate that, outside the capital city of Colombo, this was the second largest concentration of people in the country. It was also, for those few months, said to be the largest refugee camp in the world, a ground that had held out the only hope of survival for 360,000 people (UN 2012, 55; Weiss 2011, 206).

No soundtrack of hovering aircraft or shock of heavy munitions accompanies the over-seeing satellite scenographies of Mullivaikkal. One commentator, indeed, describes these soundless frames as 'much like a cartoon' (Weiss 2011, 206). The pixelation of these silent, depthless images were deliberately formulated by Google Earth so as to obscure any view of a human body (Weizman and Manfredi 2013, 186). Atrocity and suffering on this human scale remain *structurally* imperceptible in the over-sight of the orbital gaze. Yet what is still represented in these images is a stark and shocking violence, visited on a seemingly unpeopled landscape. This is a violence that unfolds spatially—literally on the ground—as well as temporally in the relation of one frame to one another; its violence resides as much on what happens between the frames, in their very sequentiality. Direct on-screen evidence of the violence visited on human bodies also exists, but it would not surface until far too late. In these disembodied satellite scenographies, with their broken constellations of dots and blips, no screams are heard from the dying, nor the anguished wailing of their bereaved, no vulgar traces of blood or shattered bodies: just a god's eye view of a massacre in progress.

The satellite images of Mullivaikkal have haunted me for many months, for what they show of the ground of massacre and for what they do not. Here the biopolitics of global governance play out across necropolitical terrains of geopolitical inequality, bringing the materiality of slaughtered bodies and the suffering of survivors into view within a spatial and specular order in which mass violence and atrocity are ever more available to be surveilled, recorded, archived, and forensically analysed, and yet, paradoxically, are rendered ever more incidental, instrumental or ignorable in relation to lives coded as expendable, under TIC's supervisory purview.

DOI: 10.1057/9781137444646.0010

Lawfare and the economies of atrocity

Compiling witness accounts from The Cage after the LTTE's defeat, the highly respected group University Teachers for Human Rights (Jaffna) (UTHR [J]) wrote: 'what these survivors' stories make clear is that for both parties, the key to military knowledge lay not in brilliant strategies, but in an utter disregard for the lives of civilians and combatants alike' (2009, 1).[1] The strategies of both warring parties recklessly wagered the lives of the civilians in The Cage on the response of the international community. At stake for each side was the very idea of a separate Tamil homeland. The Lanka government wagered, correctly as it turned out, that it could act with impunity to unleash indiscriminate violence against the inhabitants of The Cage, banking on TIC's stance on the war on terror, and backed both by the staunch support of its major arms supplier, China, and the direct and indirect support of the US (Anderson 2011). Thus, while speaking of 'humanitarian rescue' of 'hostages', the government adopted a strategy under which 'the entire people was shelled and bombed' across the region and into The Cage (UTHR [J] 2009, 19). A campaign of brutal rape, as discussed in Chapter 5, formed a part of these tactics. A UN official testified later that 'a large number of women fleeing from the conflict areas during the peak of fighting were sexually assaulted', causing civilians 'to flee back to the theater of conflict to escape the abuse' by the army (HRW 2013, 7). Through these means, the state carried out a deliberate strategy of terror and violent displacement of the civilian Tamil population, including children, the ill, the vulnerable and the elderly, into zones where they came under fire, 'as though to dispel any notion in their minds that the land belonged to them' (UTHR [J] 2009, 19).

On the LTTE's part, its strategy was based on the deadly miscalculation, as it turned out, that the spectacle of dead and wounded civilians would result in an eleventh-hour diplomatic intervention. To this end, it not only brutally exposed non-combatants to the government's brutal violence, but even sought to incite it, through means such as firing from amid civilian enclaves. The callous indifference demonstrated by the LTTE towards the lives of the Tamil population it claimed to represent was not a final resort *in extremis*, but part of its continuing tactics. A poem by Rajani Thiranagama, written at the time of the LTTE's battles with the Indian forces in the 1990s, is frighteningly prescient:

DOI: 10.1057/9781137444646.0010

Our great defenders and freedom fighters
lure the enemy right to our door-step
to the inside of the hospital
start a fight,...
And then come the shells, whizzing, whizzing.
Bloody hell,
Tigers have withdrawn, while
We, the sacrificial lambs
Drop dead in lots.

(Thiranagama, quoted by Sumathy 2004, 145)

Although some apologists for the LTTE would claim a revolutionary, Fanonian, character to its violence, and assert that its downfall was caused by requiring from it an impossible level of compliance with the norms and conventions of international law (Malathy 2012), the LTTE project had lost any liberatory or revolutionary energies it had commanded since at least the late 1980s (Hoole et al. 1990; Manikkalingam 1995; UTHR [J] 2009; Hoole 2015). Tellingly, in the final days, selected senior members of the LTTE leadership even hatched a plan, with the aid of international journalists and diplomats, for their own rescue, with a shocking indifference to the fate of those they planned to leave behind. The Lankan government's clear violation of international law in failing to honour the surrender of these LTTE leaders under a white flag has been rightly widely reported and condemned as an instance of unlawful killing (UN 2102, 86; ICEP 2014 v). However, there is no denying the shocking indifference of these leading LTTE figures to the fate of those they planned to abandon, while negotiating safe passage for themselves and their families. During this same period, LTTE cadres forcibly prevented civilians, including families, the wounded and the dying, who sought to surrender or flee to government territory from doing so on pain of death (UTHR [J] 2009; ICEP 2013).[2]

Staked on the limit-points and thresholds that constitute international humanitarian law (IHL), the tactics of a cruel indifference to the human toll adopted by both sides approximate to a form of lawfare, under which warring parties weigh up the odds of killing or saving lives against the legal definitions, categories and limits that delineate crimes against humanity. In such instances, Weizman remarks, 'the "law making character" inherent in military violence' becomes evident, as the boundaries of the laws of war are tested and extended (2011, 94). The ability to mobilise public opinion is critical to such lawfare, and to the ways in which the conflict is perceived, both in real-time and in retrospect.

DOI: 10.1057/9781137444646.0010

In the last phase of the war and for months after, the Lankan government maintained that it had carried out a 'humanitarian operation' with a policy of 'zero civilian casualties' in the No Fire Zone (Ministry of Defence, Sri Lanka 2010). The UN, for all intents and purposes, accepted these egregious assertions at face value, maintaining a 'discreet and hopeful approach' to the Lankan state, despite overwhelming evidence to the contrary (Weiss 2011, 205; see also UN 2012). An internal UN review conducted in 2012 could not be more damning of the role played by the UN, locally and at its highest levels:

> There was a continued reluctance among UNCT [UN Country Team] institutions to stand up for the rights of the people they were mandated to assist. In Colombo, *some senior staff did not perceive the prevention of killing of civilians as their responsibility – and agency and department heads at UNHQ were not instructing them otherwise.* Seen together, the failure of the UN to…adequately confront the Government on its obstructions to humanitarian assistance, [and] to address Government responsibility for attacks that were killing civilians, collectively amounted to a failure by the UN to act within the scope of institutional mandates to meet protection responsibilities. (UN 2012, 26–7, my emphasis)

Shortly after the LTTE defeat, the UN Human Rights Commission went so far as to pass a resolution commending the Lanka government and its commitment to human rights. This was in the face of objections of its then High Commissioner for Human Rights, Navi Pillai. In marked contrast to Pillai, UN Secretary-General Ban Ki-Moon praised the government's 'tremendous efforts' (HRW 2009; UN 2012, 66–7). During Ban's visit to mark the formal end of hostilities, survivors from Mullivaikkal—held incommunicado in so-called 'welfare villages'— testified that they did not receive so much as a passing glance from the blandly smiling UN Secretary-General.

Following the government victory, Lankan army tactics were widely publicised as possible models by other states for their own internal wars. The Indian Prime Minister declared that India would adopt the 'Sri Lankan Solution' to deal with its insurgent movements within its own borders (d'Souza 2011, 13), while Pakistan and Myanmar sought its advice (Beehner 2010). Basking in its victory, the Lanka Defence Ministry conducted a three-day conference, titled 'Defeating terrorism— Sri Lankan experience' to share the secrets of its success with other states (Haviland 2011). Among the speakers was none other than David Kilcullen, an Australian army official who was chief strategist at the Office

DOI: 10.1057/9781137444646.0010

of the Coordinator for Counterterrorism in the US State Department in 2005–6, and a contributor to the US army's controversial *Field Manual 3–24, Counterinsurgency* (2006). The following year, Kilcullen would act as senior counterinsurgency advisor to General David Petraeus in Iraq. James Clad, the US Deputy Assistant Secretary of Defense for South and Southeast Asia, was also a friend of the Lankan government. According to a report in the *New Yorker*, during Clad's tenure, US satellite intelligence was 'crucial' in enabling the Lankan military to destroy the LTTE's naval fleet, the Sea Pigeons, in 2008. 'From then on, the Tigers were on the run, herded ineluctably into shrinking territory' (Anderson 2011).

Kilcullen's reflections on 'The Sri Lankan Solution' must be read in the context of the COIN operations he helped put in place for the US in Iraq and Afghanistan. His presentation at the 'Defeating Terrorism' conference included high praise for Lankan army tactics, and identified several instances of its 'best practice in counterinsurgency' (2011). Kilcullen went on to commend the ways in which the military had 'developed the soldier himself, nurturing professionalism within the army and revitalising confidence in the organisation itself' (ibid.). Delivered two years after the war's end, when the horrific abuses of rape, torture and execution had been well documented, these remarks about Lanka's successes in 'nurturing professionalism' are in keeping with official responses to the atrocities perpetrated by US forces in their COIN operations in Iraq and Afghanistan. The ways in which the practices of the US military in the war on terror licensed, and were adapted in, other conflicts in other parts of the world, still remain to be fully documented. One instance I discuss elsewhere is how the torture and abuse revealed in the Abu Ghraib images are mirrored and restaged in the trophy videos recorded by Lankan soldiers on the beaches of Mullivaikkal (Perera 2014b).

The atrocities committed at Mullivaikkal, together with the Lankan state's strategy of deliberately displacing and killing Tamil civilians, clearly instantiate Lanka's identification of itself as a superior occupying power dealing with a conquered people. Kilcullen was unequivocal in endorsing the lethal force deployed against citizens:

> The government displayed…unshakeable political will opposing all external and internal pressure for a ceasefire. That political top cover provided the time, space and support that was needed for the free execution of the strategy. The nation of Sri Lanka is very fortunate in its armed forces, but the armed forces in this case were fortunate in the political leadership that they received. (2011)

DOI: 10.1057/9781137444646.0010

Fortunate indeed, the nation that possesses both an army and a political leadership with the stomach 'for the free execution of the strategy', i.e., knowingly targeting non-combatants with murderous firepower.[3] Although Kilcullen ended his speech with standard admonitions about the need to win over the civilian population in the aftermath of the war, his speech overall strongly endorsed the Lankan state's actions.

Between the 'top-cover' provided by the Lankan political leadership, and the 'over-sight' of TIC, the civilians trapped in The Cage stood little chance. In the five years since the killing fields of Mullivaikkal, a series of reports by various international bodies details precisely the forms of violence involved in the 'free execution' of the Lankan military's counterinsurgency tactics (ICEP 2013; ICG 2010; UN 2012; HRW 2013). The accumulated disclosures, including witness testimonies and trophy videos recorded by government soldiers themselves, eventually led to a reversal of the 2009 UN Human Rights Council (HRC) resolution that congratulated the Lankan government on its victory. In 2012, 2013 and 2014, a sequence of increasingly more forceful UNHRC resolutions called for an inquiry into the war crimes committed at Mullivaikkal. TIC, which played such a critical role during the war when it lent its support to the Lankan state in the name of COIN and the global war on terror, has in the ensuing years become critical to the writing of the war into history as it comes to recognise, purportedly for the first time, 'credible evidence of war crimes' that were perpetrated in plain sight (UN 2011). These failures of the UN are itemised, as already mentioned above, with remarkable openness in the 2012 'Report Of The Secretary-General's Internal Review Panel On United Nations Action In Sri Lanka'. Although several passages of the report are redacted, it makes plain the grave failures of UN officials in fulfilling their core obligations. and further pinpoints the failures of the Security Council itself: 'The tone, content and objectives of UNHQ's engagement with Member States...were heavily influenced by what it perceived Member States wanted to hear, rather than by what Member States needed to know if they were to respond' (UN 2012, 27–8).

'A gun in one hand, the Human Rights Charter in the other'

The contradictory roles played by TIC—in the form of the United Nations, its agencies and member states—and the questions of visibility

DOI: 10.1057/9781137444646.0010

and witness to which they give rise, return again to the guiding principles on which its actions are premised, the bases of its authorising instruments, and the nature of the publics it addresses and to whom it holds itself accountable. Weizman argues that the entire apparatus of human rights, humanitarianism and international law are not separate from, but inextricably entwined with, economies of violence. and 'have become the crucial means by which the economy of violence is calculated and managed' (2011, 4). In his studies of Operation Cast Lead, the 2008–9 siege of Gaza, which he terms 'the proper noun for the horror of our humanitarian present', Weizman analyses how technologies for managing war's violence, such as 'spatial organizations and physical instruments, technical standards, and systems of monitoring', now function as 'the means for exercising contemporary violence and for governing the displaced, the enemy and the unwanted' (ibid., 4–5). Allowing states the space for, in Kilcullen's words, 'free execution of the strategy', the role of TIC becomes one of the close calibration, oversight and calculation of violence.

Caught between 'keeping violence at a low enough level to limit civilian suffering, and at a level high enough to bring a decisive end to the war and bring peace' (Weizman ibid., 9), TIC's interventions are structured by a set of 'moral technologies' for observing, measuring and managing violence. The recourse to such moral technologies in the judgements made by UN officials is clearly identified in the 2012 Internal Review as among the contributing factors in the mass deaths at Mullivaikkal. The review pinpoints the moral calculations made by officials such as:

(i) choosing not to speak up about Government and LTTE broken commitments and violations of international law was seen as *the only way to increase UN humanitarian access*;

(ii) choosing to focus briefings to the Security Council on the humanitarian situation rather than on the causes of the crisis and the obligations of the parties to the conflict was seen as a way to *facilitate constructive engagement.* (2012, 26, my emphasis)

Here, the guiding principle of identifying 'the lesser evil' in effect functions to establish thresholds of acceptability for conditions of unliveable violence and preventable death. The review names a critical distinction that needs to be made between a focus on the 'humanitarian situation' in isolation, and the identification of the political actions that are responsible for producing that 'humanitarian situation' in the first place.

DOI: 10.1057/9781137444646.0010

Weizman focuses on the 'technological continuum' between military violence and the legal and quantitative mechanisms used to assess that violence: the calculation of the 'proportionality', usually in retrospect, and, by extension, the weighing up of its levels of permissibility and legitimacy, summed up in the chilling question, 'how much is too much?' (2011, 122). What are relations between practices of accounting and the process of accountability? Do TIC's post-atrocity actuarial practices of enumerating, calculating, aggregating, balancing and summing up presume objects whose worth is commensurate to their weighty efforts? How many collateral deaths are acceptable in the execution of a targeted killing? What is the 'mathematical minimum' of homes or tents that it is permissible to reduce to rubble in order to wipe out enemy positions in a COIN operation? What are the adequate measures by which a 'voluntary human shield', who may be lawfully killed after a warning, is distinguished from a 'non-combatant' entitled to protection under international law?

In its 2014 siege of Gaza, revealingly titled Operation Protective Edge, the Israeli state responded to charges of indiscriminate bombing in its 2008 campaign by adopting practices such as the 'wake-up call'—sending warning phone or text messages to civilians prior to an attack—and the 'knock on the roof'—a preliminary strike by a missile that 'does not contain an explosive warhead' followed closely by one that did (Kishawi 2014). These tactics claiming to warn and protect, Sami Kishawi writes, had the effect of allowing 'Israel to kill two birds with one stone...It can publicly claim that it works to minimize civilian casualties while at the same time killing Palestinians...with impunity' (Kishawi 2014). The tactics Kishawi identifies strikingly parallel the corralling of the Tamil population into protective 'No Fire Zones' which in effect functioned as killing zones. As repeatedly documented, no sooner were the coordinates of field hospitals and shelters communicated to the military via international channels such as the Red Cross than they became, seemingly coincidentally, targets for shelling (Channel 4 2013). Assembled within these zones, in close proximity to the 'enemy', all civilian activities became suspect and potential targets: among those killed at Mullivaikkal were some children milling around a mobile food cart for a free sweet, and others playing on the beach for a brief respite from the bunkers (UTHR [J] 2009, 83; 62). In the space of The Cage, combatant and non-combatant, innocent and guilty, were to be distinguished only after the fact, depending on whether or not they survived. According to a statement by the Human

DOI: 10.1057/9781137444646.0010

Rights Minister, the 'soldiers saved all Tamil civilians...without shedding a drop of blood' (UTHR [J] 2009, 102). To have been killed or wounded, then, was conclusive evidence of non-civilian status, with the dead and disabled retrospectively designated legitimate targets. A statement made by the Lankan President, Mahinda Rajapaksa, takes on an even more chilling cast when considered in the context of these calculative tactics of the humanitarian present: in his commemorative speech on the second anniversary after the killings at Mullivaikkal, Rajapaksa avowed that his 'soldiers went into battle, 'carrying a gun in one hand, the Human Rights Charter in the other' (Ministry of Defence 2011).

Accounting for disposable lives

In the humanitarian present, with its collusions between humanitarian technologies, international law, political force and military power, what are the measures by which the identifiable excess between allowable and unallowable levels of deadly force is accounted for? How are target bodies of the unwanted and out-of-place at once counted and discounted in the calculus of international justice? Beginning with the satellite scenographies from Google Earth and UNOSAT, how are the dead of Mullivaikkal made available for viewing *as they are also simultaneously* rendered 'structurally invisible' in the official and unofficial fora of international justice?

The 'at risk' locations and crisis scenographies compulsively logged by global surveillance technologies cannot be dissociated from, and are already enframed and mediated by, a prior ordering of spaces, populations and life-chances, and by discursive and representational histories. Some lives register within this field of perception, while others are rendered imperceptible under its scopic and legal regimes, including those regimes mandated to prevent massacres and genocides and to protect civilians. Through what means and on what terms are these bodies and stories able to enter global view? Activist interventions, human rights discourses and popular culture all provide access to the formal mechanisms of international tribunals and resolutions, but are mediated by the need to comply with normative visual frames of war, atrocity and catastrophe. They structure the modalities in which survivor testimonies, media reconstructions and other forms of reportage of the atrocity events at Mullivaikkal were couched.

DOI: 10.1057/9781137444646.0010

It is in this context that I turn to two powerful documentaries by Callum MacRae, *Sri Lanka's Killing Fields* (2012) and *No Fire Zone* (2013), both produced by Britain's Channel 4. The productions have been highly influential in bringing the events of the war's last days to global audiences. They provided unprecedented access to the shocking trophy videos made by Lankan soldiers, as well as to the footage compiled by LTTE media teams, who risked their own lives to inform the world. Raw, pointed, partisan, MacRae's documentaries are primarily addressed to an international audience of opinion-makers. The films are clearly aimed at achieving a UN Resolution and international inquiry into the atrocities of Mullivaikkal, and in fact were screened at the UN prior to the 2014 debate on Lanka. The voices most frequently heard in them are those of global NGO workers, international experts or diaspora—mostly pro-LTTE—Tamils fluent in English.

The opening sequence of *No Fire Zone* sets the scene for the narrative that follows: a series of children's hands thrust pleadingly through a gap in the locked gates of a UN compound, while inside TIC plans its withdrawal from the 'humanitarian situation' that is unfolding. The hands, small, brown, disembodied, are accompanied by a low keening, a voiceless plea not to be abandoned. As the convoy of SUVs speeds away, seemingly helpless in the face of the Lankan government's decree to evacuate, a voiceover by an international (white) UN spokesperson articulates his sense of frustration at the inability to accede to the children's pleading. Framed by this scene of the international failure to protect the innocent, to have *done something*, the documentary is a ringing call for an international justice that will keep faith, if belatedly, with those it failed, and redress the shameful act of abandonment of nearly five years before. The narrative's logic is one of exposure and shaming of TIC in the name of the dead and the survivors. This shame can be said to have been partially assuaged when, on 27 March 2014, the UNHRC finally did something: it voted to open an international investigation into possible war crimes by both the Lankan government and LTTE forces.

The March 2014 Resolution is in this sense a vindication for the activists who sought to bring the events at Mullivaikkal to global visibility, and a moment of self-redemption for TIC, in light of its initial act of abandonment. The scenes of shameful retreat are already familiar to global audiences from various accounts of the UN's role

DOI: 10.1057/9781137444646.0010

in Bosnia, such as the withdrawal from Srebrenica, or in fictionalised versions through films such as *Hotel Rwanda*. Yet, the trope of TIC's shaming, its failure to *do something*, Randall Williams argues, works in complex ways that leave broader geopolitical relations untouched. He asks: 'what if shaming operations promote, however unwittingly and unintentionally, a necessary misrecognition of geopolitics and power that renders them largely ineffective as an anti-imperialist political platform?' (2010, 46). Williams goes on to examine the narrative of the UN's shaming in *Hotel Rwanda* as a move by which TIC disowns its prior responsibilities for the past and present, as it authorises more intervention for the future.

Building on Williams' argument, I would argue that the moment of TIC's turning away is simultaneously the moment at which, through the staging of the International Community's failure, 'humanitarian situations' come to be identified as such. In this moment of marking the 'humanitarian situation' as exceptional, a breakdown of the international order, the moment of crisis is marked also as the moment when that crisis is implicitly resolved, through the invocation of *future* measures of redress. The shameful moment of international withdrawal sets the scene for the series of subsequent inquiries, reports, tribunals, resolutions and sanctions to follow, through which the principle of accountability for disposable lives will be performed, reinstating the status of international law and human rights as the custodians of those very rights, *even at the moment of their breakdown*. TIC's moment of shaming before the victim of humanitarian catastrophe then, is a necessary moment in which a necro-geopolitical order proactively reaffirms itself.

Return to the lagoon's edge

As the passing of the UNHRC Resolution on 27 March 2014 registers the success of the first phase of call for international accountability, I return to the battlefields at the edge of the Nanthikadal lagoon. Walking this scorched ground in the days after the battle, the narrator of UTHR[J], a tireless and unwavering witness to the prolonged carnage of this 30-year war, spoke of 'the still eloquence of wastelands', of the earth harrowed by craters and mines, littered with fragments of shells and cluster bombs,

DOI: 10.1057/9781137444646.0010

and marked by the fragile and broken remnants of human presence (UTHR [J] 2009, 8).

Five years later, this massacre ground has become, incredibly, the site of a luxury hotel operated by the Lankan military, while doubling as the Security Forces HQ for the region. The hotel, 'Lagoon's Edge', is literally built on the bodies and bones of those who died at Mullivaikkal. The grounds are landscaped with replicas and crude monuments to the war. Its kitsch appearance is reminiscent of the simulacra produced by the retired Indonesian mass murderers of 1965–6 in Joshua Oppenheimer's acclaimed 2012 film, *The Art of Killing* (Perera 2014a). As in Suharto's Indonesia, a new order has been initiated in Lanka following an era of mass violence. Its attendant features are lavish display and visual excess, summed up by Sumathy as an aesthetics of triumphalism (2014). Advertisements and billboards dominate this landscape; its monuments are gleaming shopping malls, luxury hotels and revived monuments of a mythic Sinhala heritage.

The Lagoon's Edge Hotel reinforces the triumph of what Sumathy describes as the militarising gaze that imposes itself, not in only in the occupation of the former war zone, but throughout the land:

> The militarising gaze is also a consuming gaze, accompanied by a certain glitz and glamour. City gentrification programmes are underway, displacing the urban poor. Boutique hotels, coffee shops, night bazaars...take racy nightlife styles...to the streets...Mega construction projects connect cities through expressways...and newly reconstructed roads are able to take a visitor deep into the interior where boutique hotels and resorts [proliferate]. (ibid.)

This form of neoliberal militarisation, with its aura of global glitz and glamour, its massive construction projects and booming tourist and heritage trade, complements and consolidates the military occupation of the north and, in Wijeyeratne's words, the technologies aimed at the 'existential encompassment' of Tamils and other minoritised subjects (2012, 403). As the military gaze is normalised throughout the land, the opposition to an international inquiry into the killings has become less strident. The diplomat who led Lanka's successful campaign to foil a condemnatory resolution by the UN in 2009 has been quietly removed, to return as a soft critic of the regime; other government apologists, too, have moderated their defence of the indefensible, and turned to pre-war nostalgia. Despite some predictable outcry at the 2014 resolution, there

DOI: 10.1057/9781137444646.0010

appears to be a level of recognition in ruling circles that the price of rehabilitation into the international order may be a form of cooperation with an international inquiry.

The presidential election of January 2015 resulted in the shock defeat of Rajapaksa. A former minister of his cabinet is now president. While some moves by the new government, such as the replacement of the military governor of Jaffna by a civilian, are promising, the continuing presence of several members of the former government suggests that this is the 'moderate' face of regime change. Meanwhile, many LTTE supporters, too, have adopted new faces, remaking themselves in the image of the defenders of human rights. As the Tamil-Canadian commentator D.B.S. Jeyaraj observed wryly:

> Ostensibly the name of the LTTE game [is]...now a lofty quest for justice, accountability, reconciliation and equality. A tragic-comic aspect of the changed scenario was the spectacle of accredited representatives from respected human rights organizations associating with yesteryear tigers...The battlefront had seemingly shifted to the UN Human Rights Council arena in the new venue of Geneva. (2014)

As I have attempted to show, accountability through the fora of international justice has been not only delayed, but fatally compromised and deformed by its own processes. In the Humanitarian Present, the prospect of a forthcoming international investigation into the war represents yet another compromising victory for the lesser evil, one in which the most culpable parties on both sides remain unscathed: an accounting in which the disposable lives of Mullivaikkal yet remain discounted.

Notes

1   There are no definitive figures for the death toll, and estimates range from 40,000–110,000. Following UTHR (J), an organisation that has fearlessly chronicled the history of the war since the early 1980s, I adopt the minimum estimate of 40,000 casualties (2009, 115). In his later analysis, Rajan Hoole of UTHR (J) presents a more detailed breakdown of the figures, amounting to 97,000 civilian losses, of which 67,600 are attributed to Lankan security forces and 23,000 to LTTE actions (Hoole 2015, 228).

DOI: 10.1057/9781137444646.0010

2   A witness in the No Fire Zone estimated that 'about 25% of the civilian casualties in the NFZ, averaging about 15–20 a day, were of people killed by the LTTE when trying to escape' (UTHR [J] 2009b, 67).

3   These remarks were later removed from some published versions of Kilcullen's speech, but remain in others, and in the YouTube recording of his address.

DOI: 10.1057/9781137444646.0010

5

Territory of Ashes: A Disjointed Unfolding

Abstract: *Chapter 5 discusses the acts of mass rape-torture that followed the LTTE's defeat. It attempts to situate the multivalent figure of the LTTE female cadre, most often imagined as a suicide bomber, within discursive economies of gender, nationalism and terror.*

Keywords: agonal sovereignty; horrorism; rape in war; suicide bomber; Tamil Tigress

Perera, Suvendrini. *Survival Media: The Politics and Poetics of Mobility and the War in Sri Lanka.* New York: Palgrave Macmillan, 2016. DOI: 10.1057/9781137444646.0011.

> *Stones fill the mouth*
> *Weigh down the tongue*
>
> (Jean Arasanayagam, 'Rendition')

'Let Them Speak', the University Teachers for Human Rights (Jaffna) (UTHR [J]) report on the last days of the war, presents a horrific scene on the banks of the Nanthikadal lagoon on 16 May 2009, a day before the official surrender of the LTTE. The passage cites eyewitness accounts of the plight of the LTTE's famous female cadres, once believed by many of its proponents to represent its best liberationist energies for a new society (Balasingham 1993). On 14 May, when the approaching defeat could be no longer denied, these girls and women—conscripts and volunteers alike—were discharged from their roles by their all-male leadership (UTHR [J] 2009, 89). By 16 May, those who had families or friends among the civilians had reunited with them and joined the throngs seeking to flee into government territory ahead of the final battle.

The wounded and helpless who had no means of escape found themselves exposed and desperate as the Lankan army closed in for its final assault. 'Among the most tragic sights were hundreds of young injured LTTE cadres, many of them girls, who were brought early in the morning… and stretched out along the sides of the road near the southern end of the NFZ', UTHR (J) recounts (2009, 95). Their leaders had expected that the military would allow the International Red Cross safe access to evacuate these wounded fighters. No rescue eventuated, but the women were left lying in the open, unable to move:

> The victims who had lost limbs and some their sight were by evening screaming in agony, begging for someone to take them along or at least to give them a cyanide capsule. A ten year old boy searched the road for cyanide capsules and gave them to some of the injured cadres…The cadres who survived the fighting…had abandoned their cyanide capsules and uniforms, put on civilian clothes and joined the exodus with their families. That was how there were plenty of cyanide capsules along the roadsides. On the previous day when the LTTE had begun setting fire to their equipment, a number of cadres, especially women, who had disabilities due to injury, had cast themselves into the flames. (ibid.)

I have come across no more hellish images than these among the many shocking testimonies that have emerged from the teeming chaos and carnage of the LTTE's final hours: cast-off suicide capsules strewn along the ground, as some of the more fortunate among the women fling away their old identities to escape across the lagoon; the pleading cries of the blinded and maimed left behind as they begged for the means to end their

DOI: 10.1057/9781137444646.0011

lives; a child of ten taking pity on their plight and stopping to scrabble for vials of cyanide thrown by the roadside; the inferno of the previous night, when wounded girls and women cast themselves alive into the flames alongside their arms, rather than face capture. Even as these scenes of horror test the limits of my understanding, fill the mouth with stones, they are not to be avoided in explorations of diasporic Tamil subjectivities. The stories of these female cadres emerging at first through diasporic networks and brought to global attention, outline crucial dimensions of the conflict, the virulent logic that directed it on all sides, and the destructive forces that continue to play out in its unresolved aftermath, even as they continue to harrow the consciousness of diasporic and refugee subjects, and shape their practices of memory and forgetting, their politics of self-understanding and protest, critique and survival.

A witness who saw the lines of pleading, helpless girls laid out on the ground describes himself as being 'moved with deep sadness and guilt' at the sight. 'These cadres were very young and they were not sufficiently developed to understand the world around them and the nature of their fate. Their organization should never have allowed them to suffer in this manner' (UTHR[J] 2009, 108). This oblique reference to the 'nature of their fate' can be amplified by reference to the documented evidence of rape and torture that has surfaced since the war (ICEP 2014; HRW 2013; *No Fire Zone* 2014). Some accounts of these final months indicate that acts of mass rape and extreme sexual violence were not incidental aberrations in this conflict, but were integral to the military tactics of the state. As quoted in Chapter 4, a former UN field worker reported that the fear of rape had motivated a large number of civilians seeking to escape into government territory to 'flee back to the theater of conflict to escape the abuse' (HRW 2013, 7). This suggests that the practice of rape-torture by state forces contributed to the high number of casualties in the final battle, as well being responsible for uncounted numbers of deaths and incidences of violence and atrocity that followed it. I adopt the term rape-torture to mark the extremes of violent brutality that characterised these acts. While the state and its supporters continue to deny the incidence of mass rape by the army, they do so in half-hearted and unconvincing fashion (e.g., Marga Institute 2014). Despite these denials, the weight of evidence is documented in a sequence of personal testimonies and independent reports (ICEP 2014; HRW 2013; UTHR [J] 2009). Like the bombing of civilians described in Chapter 4, these are tactics linked to deeply held ideologies of ethnoreligious supremacy

DOI: 10.1057/9781137444646.0011

that shaped the forms of warfare adopted by the state and its agents. At the same time, the threat or fear of rape by the army was a constant thematic in LTTE rhetoric, functioning to mobilise both women and men into its ranks and to rationalise and justify representations of the LTTE as the patriarchal guardian and sole protector of Tamil women and nationhood (Maunaguru 1995; Sumathy 2004; Coomaraswamy and Perera-Rajasingham 2009; Satkunananthan 2012).

A certain horror

The scenes of the wounded LTTE women on the banks of Nanthikadal, as they plead for cyanide to put an end their hopeless situation, recall an exchange from one of the most sympathetic accounts of these fighters: the documentary, *My Daughter the Terrorist*. Made by Norwegian filmmaker Beate Arnestad two years before the defeat of the LTTE, *My Daughter the Terrorist* presents the story of Dharshika, a girl who ran away from her mother to join the LTTE at the age of 12, after her father had been killed in a government aerial raid on the Jaffna Post Office. Dharshika and her friend Puhalchudhar are proud and fiercely loyal members of the Black Tigers suicide squad. Their stories evoke both the unshakable conviction and the fierce desperation that govern the lives and deaths of these young fighters. At the time of filming, the women, both now in their twenties, are veterans of several combat missions, and say that they have killed many soldiers. In a rare reflective moment, they sit on a river bank, admiring a vista on the other side where trees, hills and sky coalesce into a still, far horizon. Giggling and joking, they tell the film-maker about the sights that confront them whenever they shut their eyes. In these dream scenarios, the guns they're carrying suddenly refuse to fire. The government soldiers they're shooting at refuse to die. Instead, the soldiers advance ever closer towards them, wave after wave. At this point, one of the young women breaks the nightmare mood. *A good thing we don't bite down on our cyanide capsules during these dreams*, she quips, *or we would never wake up!* In between giggles, they explain, carefully, how the capsules are supposed to work: biting down on the glass would cut into their tongues, allowing the poison to enter the bloodstream and killing them instantly. They add: if we're too injured to bite, we just need to empty the capsule directly into our wounds. Then it would be all right. They smile reassuringly for the interviewer, and perhaps themselves.

DOI: 10.1057/9781137444646.0011

We know that Dharshika, at least, did not die at Mullivaikkal, but some years earlier, in combat. *My Daughter, The Terrorist* ends with the scene of Dahrshika's mother grieving for her at the ceremonial gravesite the LTTE ordains for its *marveerar*, the great heroes who die in suicide missions. These cemeteries have since been razed by the victorious Lankan state. No commemorative gravestones either for the LTTE cadres, female or male, who died at Mullivaikkal two years later. Little information is available on their numbers or the manner of their deaths. Some cadres surrendered to the military in full view of witnesses, but were not seen again in the 'welfare villages' at Manik Farm, where prisoners and 'surrendees', as they are known, were held. No figures exist of those raped, tortured or executed in cold blood, although a number of international reports give extensive accounts of the conduct of rape and other forms of torture at these sites (HRW 2013, ICEP 2014).

Apart from the first-person accounts by survivors and aid workers, a relatively new form of information on the female cadres' fate at Mullivaikkal has emerged in fragments of blurry trophy videos and triumphal selfies from the battlefield. Recorded by victorious soldiers on their mobile phones are nightmarish images of piles of naked female bodies, hacked and mutilated. The bodies are casually flung on the back of a truck as soldiers banter and laugh among themselves. 'This one has the best figure', one remarks of a naked and bruised corpse. A cell phone video aired on Channel 4 reveals a figure known to many Lankan and diaspora audiences as the LTTE newsreader and singer, Isaipriya, who reportedly held the rank of Lieutenant-Colonel in the LTTE (ICEP 2014, 132). Dazed and distraught, clearly in pain, hardly able to walk, she comes into view, dragging herself through the shallow lagoon. Her upper body is completely uncovered; sodden pants of some pale, flimsy material cling to her legs. As the camera records, a group of soldiers helps her out of the water. They cover her torso with a white cloth. We hear them identifying her, in Sinhala, as the daughter of Prabhakaran, the LTTE leader. 'I am not her!' she cries, in Tamil. Her voice sounds thick and agonised, despairing. The soldiers lead her away, out of camera range (Channel 4 2013). On a different phone video, the same woman appears again. Now she is a corpse, naked and ashen. There is a bloody gash across her face. Another dead woman, her shirt lifted to her neck, lies next to her in the mud. It is unclear whether the women were found in that position or posed there for the trophy shot.

DOI: 10.1057/9781137444646.0011

From yet another photograph, the International Crimes Evidence Project provides the following clinical description:

> ICEP has collected additional photographs that depict a scene with seven naked or partly clad individuals, one of whom is Isaipriya, lying on her back. Six of the individuals have ligatures, and five have blindfolds around their faces. None of these individuals are wearing military-style uniforms. Independent analysis by a forensic pathologist... indicates that blood patterns are consistent with the death of persons depicted in the photographs as occurring at the scene... According to this forensic pathologist, Isaipriya may have had her hands bound behind her back. She appears to have blood across her face. Her shirt is bloodied and is bunched at her neck, exposing her right breast. She is wearing light brown coloured trousers, similar to those depicted in the video described above. A white cloth that could be the same cloth depicted in the Channel 4 video... [is] loosely placed over her stomach and waist, covering her genitals. Her underwear appears to have been completely removed from her left leg and rests on her right leg adjacent to her trousers, which have been pulled down to her knees. (ICEP 2014, 169)

The visual and verbal accounts from within and around the No Fire Zone in early 2009 indicate that the level of sexual violence perpetrated there was both unbridled in its savagery and staggering in its extent. '*When rape is authorized by conquest*', Jean Franco writes in her study of rape in the Peruvian and Guatemalan civil wars, '*there are no limits*' (2013, 15). Despite the publicity that has attached to Isaipriya's horrific death, what was done to her at Mullivaikkal was not exceptional, as the bodies lying next to her demonstrate. Research gathered by the International Crimes Evidence Project for a report commissioned by the reputable Australian Public Interest Advocacy Centre, states that hundreds of other women, not publicly recognisable in the same way, were also raped and killed even before the final battle at Mullivaikkal:

> A local employee of an international agency identified the mortuary at a Government Hospital as the holding place of large numbers of bodies of deceased and mutilated Tamil women in February and March 2009. He observed at least 200 bodies, of mainly Tamil women and young girls, on three or four occasions when he visited the facility... He reported that many of the bodies of the women were naked and bore physical evidence of rape and sexual mutilation, with knife wounds in the nature of long slashes, bite marks or deep scratches on the breasts, and vaginal mutilation by knives, bottles and sticks. The bodies also typically bore signs of gunshot wounds to the forehead, which appeared to have been inflicted at close range due to the lack of peripheral damage. (ICEP 2014, 157)

DOI: 10.1057/9781137444646.0011

'To rape and then kill', in Franco's analysis, 'suggests more than an act of warrior triumph' (2013, 79). The killing of those who had been raped, and the raping of those who had been killed, were atrocities that also occurred in the conflicts in Peru and Guatemala. These, among others, Franco notes, are acts of savage supremacy calculated to annihilate the subjectivity of the defeated: 'Rape followed by execution performs expulsion from the human by first reducing subjects to a state of abjection and then disposing of them as so much rubbish...rape not only abolishes any claim by the victim to be in the same "human" category as the rapist, who is confirmed in his supremacy but also annihilates the woman as the feared other' (ibid., 78). The acts of rape, torture, murder and mutilation visited on conquered bodies reduces them to a state of so much waste, shapeless matter to be disposed of. In her influential book, *Horrorism*, Adriana Cavarero similarly describes the form of violence 'that, not content merely to kill...aims to destroy the uniqueness of the body, tearing at its constitutive vulnerability' (2009, 8). This is violence characterised by a 'certain horror' (Debrix and Barder 2012, 24). It operates at the level of 'the savaging of the body as body', its destruction as a 'figural unity' (Cavarero 2009, 80).

In their commentary on Cavarero's text, Francois Debrix and Alexander D. Barder link this form of annihilating violence to what they name 'agonal sovereignty' as a 'form of power and violence that embraces horror', and in which 'traditional...biopolitical distinctions between...law-creating and law-maintaining order, on the one hand, and unbounded violence, on the other, are no longer operative' (2012, 21). Confronted by the annihilating violence of horrorism, the spectator is transfixed, immobilised. Agonal sovereignty is characterised by its excess, by 'overkill' (ibid., 122). It exceeds traditional theoretical frameworks of sovereignty and biopolitics, although 'agonal sovereignty is one that may appear to start with biopolitical elements' as it proceeds to 'transmute the biopolitical into an ultra-negative ontology of being or of the human' (ibid., 22). The targets of this type of excess are no longer 'human subjects, citizens, selves'— life, humanity, species—but 'body parts, fragments of lives, bits and pieces of singular human experience and...their always readily reopened wounds and scars'. This is a form of sovereignty that seeks to 'dismantle' and disjoint and that 'indiscriminately mutilates bodies as much as it arbitrarily traumatizes minds and psyches', operating across cognitive and sensory registers (ibid.).

DOI: 10.1057/9781137444646.0011

As Debrix and Barder elaborate: 'biopolitical frames of representability are epistemological frames that render intelligible practices of power and violence in terms of preservation of life, a preservation of life that sometimes entails the possibility of taking away the lives or destroying the bodies of others (unworthy bodies or lives)' (ibid.,120). A number of theorists have suggested that these Foucauldian biopolitical frameworks need to be extended to account for a biopolitics of extreme violence and slaughter. Mbembe's necropolitics, Cavarero's 'horrorism' and Debrix and Barder's 'agonal sovereignty' may all be seen as attempts to theorise the excess of sovereign violence. Cavarero identifies horrorism as a form of sovereignty characterised by its sheer excess of violence: a violence that is designed to immobilise and paralyse, and one that is constitutively gendered. Where terror is mobile, and sets us in motion, Cavarero writes, horror stops us in our tracks; it arrests us with its spectacular violence, transfixes us by the sight of its severed and bloody Gorgon's head (2009, 14). Horrorism is characterised by the sheer useless excess, even exuberance, of its violence: its overkill. Its favoured modes are the visual and the symbolic. There is 'a daring, challenging, defiant and recreative aspect to horror and horrific violence'; indeed a 'recreational' aspect (Debrix and Barder 2012, 35): the defiant, performative revelry on view in the trophy videos of Lankan soldiers posing with massed naked and mutilated women's corpses.

What are the means by which to respond to the transfixing and immobilising effects of a sovereign violence of excess, overkill and horror? To avoid paralysis before the annihilating gaze of the Gorgon? Debrix and Barder propose a mirroring of its horrific excesses, a reflecting that aims not to recover or remake the bodies and lives unmade by an excess of sovereign violence, but to respond to dismembering violence by a 'disjointed unfolding' and 'an ethic of inventorying the scattered' (ibid., 130).

Rape-torture and the lethal logics of sovereignty

In the context of the savage torture-rapes of the war, the explanatory frameworks I muster in this scattered unfolding reflect on a combination among forms of sovereign violence, biopolitical and agonal, punitive and annihilating, historical and contemporary, performative and expressive. Franco notes in her account of the torture-rapes in Peru and Guatemala that the women raped by the military were overwhelmingly

DOI: 10.1057/9781137444646.0011

indigenous: 'Is it too exaggerated to suggest that it is a re-enactment of the Conquest itself...that it attempted to finish the work of conquest?' (2013, 79). The reference to the conquest positions these torture-rapes in a historical framework within which colonial mastery is viewed not as a singular event or accomplishment, but as an act that must be continually reiterated and re-enacted in the present, a compulsive embodied restaging of the violent claim to sovereignty over conquered subjects and territory. In acts of rape and torture perpetrated by the Indian army in Kashmir, a similar logic of sovereignty is operative (Bora 2010; Dutta 2013). When soldiers of the Indian army commit acts of rape, Abhijit Dutta argues, 'they are doing their duty, they are teaching "them" a lesson, they are keeping Kashmir "integral" to India' (2013). In 1997, in Amparai in Eastern Lanka, in a particularly horrific instance of dismembering violence, Koneswary, a young woman, was raped and mutilated by a grenade thrust into her vagina (Nuhman 2012; Sumathy forthcoming). Her torture-rape is a link in a chain of annihilating violence that included the rape and murder of a 17-year-old schoolgirl, Krishanthi Kumaraswamy, in Jaffna, of the pregnant Wijikala Nanthan and Sivamani Sinnathamby in Mannar, and many others to this day.

That the savage rapes and mutilations by the Lankan forces did not end with the war, but continued, both inside the 'welfare villages' and outside them, indicates a similar motivation to that mooted by Franco, Dutta and others: of torture-rape as part of a continuing violent staging of sovereignty upon the bodies of conquered subjects. Many of the torture-rapes documented in the Human Rights Watch report make no pretence of having a tactical objective in view, such as obtaining a confession or gaining information. Rather, their motivation is summed up in the quotation by a Lankan army officer that forms the title of the HRW report: 'We will teach you a lesson'. Dutta deploys the identical phrase in her analysis of rape by the Indian army in Kashmir. An account by KN is representative of the experiences documented in the HRW report on Lanka:

> We were taken to Omanthai on April 21, 2009. All of us were stripped naked. The soldiers asked all the women and men to bend over and laughed when we did. They groped us and felt our breasts. On April 22, a bus took us to Arunachalam camp at Chettikulam Vavuniya...I shared the tent with six other young women. Each of us was invited for an inquiry. The officials who conducted the inquiry wore military uniforms. The inquiry happened only at night time. The officials who interrogated me took turns to rape me. They took

DOI: 10.1057/9781137444646.0011

my photographs and fingerprints. They asked about my husband's whereabouts and how he supported the LTTE. I told them I didn't know anything. They slapped me and then said they would fix me. They raped me by turn. There were four or five people. I went back to my tent after they finished. They would call different girls from the tent and I was called at least six times. They did not ask me to sign a confession document. (HRW 2013, 114)

'They slapped me and then said they would fix me': The mass rapes to which KN and her fellow prisoners are subjected are characterised as practices of corporeal discipline administered to the recalcitrant subject. As a form of torture that is not 'productive' (Pugliese 2013, 1–3) in yielding information or seeking a confession, the rape of KN is not instrumental, but an end in itself, a 'lesson' in subjection validated by the sovereign will to power assumed by these agents of the state.

We Will Teach You A Lesson presents 75 interviews with survivors who were subject to torture-rape and sexual violence while they were held in state custody, prior to, during and after the last stage of the war in Lanka. The survivors were all interviewed outside Lanka, and their accounts were corroborated in almost every instance by medical practitioners who saw evidence of the physical and mental effects of the abuse described. Unlike the cases of Peru and Guatemala, those who were subjected to rape by Lankan security forces included men as well as women. Of the 75 cases interviewed for the HRW report, 41 were women, 31 were men and 3 were boys under 18. Even allowing for the fact that many women would have held back from reporting their rapes, the relatively high proportion of male victims is notable. After considering the incidence and contexts of these rapes committed against women, men and minors, the authors of the report reach the conclusion, 'In short, there appears to be no category of Tamil who, once taken into custody, is immune from rape and other sexual violence' (HRW 2013, 36). The understanding arrived at by Human Rights Watch situates the Tamil subject, regardless of gender, as one who is available to be raped. In the cause of asserting the indivisibility and integrity of state of Lanka, bodies seen as opposing that doctrine are available to be indiscriminately split open, rent apart, in the assertion of the inviolable sovereignty of the state.

Understood as 'expressive crimes', crimes in which the bodies of those killed illustrate the logic of the killers (Franco 2013, 21), the torture-rapes of Tamil women and men instantiate the violent logic of an ultimate exercise of sovereignty, an assertion of a heteronormative mastery over the subjugated through which aspirations of separatism are rebutted in this

DOI: 10.1057/9781137444646.0011

most violent act of incorporation by the other. The crime of rape-torture must be read as expressive of the logic of the Sinhala state's sovereignty as a form of 'ultra-negative ontology' (Debrix and Barder 2012, 22) within which Tamils, along with others excluded from ethnoreligious or class supremacy, can only ever occupy a subordinate and subjugated position in the nation. Tamils and other minoritised citizens, such as Muslims, Sinhala Catholics and Christians and the rural and working poor, who are excluded from the centre of cultural power, signify as lesser figures at best, and interlopers at worst, in the framework of supremacist Sinhala-Buddhist ontotopology: that is, the linking of an ontological state of being with a '*topos* of territory, native soil, city, body in general' (Derrida 1993, 82). As argued in previous chapters, the assumption of Sinhala sovereign authority over a naturalised territorial entity, the island of 'Sri Lanka', is buttressed by an ensemble of politico-cultural forces, including the practice of a Buddhist biopolitics in the spaces and activities of everyday life, a set of spatial-geographical technologies that sanction the belief in Lanka as the chosen land for the protection of Buddhism, and an educational project that validates a mythic view of the Sinhala as a race apart (Krishna 1999; Ismail 2005; Wijeyaratne 2012). Perceived challenges to the secondary place assigned to Tamils, Muslims, and other non-Buddhists in this imagined ethnoreligious hierarchy is met with a 'lesson' designed to publicly instruct and chastise, as it ultimately dismembers and annihilates through its punitive display of the infliction of extreme violence.

Rapeable subjects

Throughout the Lankan war, the perpetration of rape and sexual violence is agreed to have been markedly 'asymmetric' (Wood 2009, 143). From its inception, the LTTE carried out numerous targeted executions and atrocities, organised deliberate, indiscriminate bombings in public places, which killed and maimed thousands of non-combatants, and also perpetrated massacres of entire Sinhala and Muslim villages in border zones. Yet it is generally agreed that sexual assault and rape did not form part of its 'repertoire' of terror (Wood 2009). Rape—both within and outside LTTE ranks—was strictly prohibited by the leadership, and virtually no reports exist of rape by LTTE cadres (ibid., 152). However, the LTTE did engage in other forms of gendered violence, including the

DOI: 10.1057/9781137444646.0011

murder of those deemed to have transgressed sexually—transgender people, Tamil women who partnered with Sinhala men or were deemed to have violated norms of dress and decorum, cadres exposed in sexual relationships—and also tolerated or ignored the violence perpetrated by its male cadres against both female cadres and other women (Sumathy forthcoming; Satkunanathan 2012). Most commentators attribute the asymmetry in the infliction of torture-rape and sexual violence to the stringent discipline exercised by the LTTE, as well as to the mores of Tamil society—although there is little to indicate any higher tolerance of rape in Sinhala society. More insightfully, Sumathy locates the LTTE's 'public emphasis on [rigidly controlling] the sexuality of its cadres, both men and women' as a meshing of the repressive sexual mores of Jaffna society with the LTTE's totalising investment in a 'centralized command and politics of renunciation' (2004, 129–30). When it became clear that defeat was inevitable, however, this iron discipline apparently broke down. In an account cited by Hoole, a witness asserts that 'in its last days the LTTE committed unspeakable crimes on female conscripts, often as part of the terms for letting them escape' (2015, 147).

The commitment to a repressive 'politics of renunciation' that defined the LTTE for the greatest part of its existence is embodied in the figure of its female cadres. As symbols of a future Tamil nation, female cadres occupied a prominent place in the LTTE's own mythology (Balasingham 1993), while attracting a high degree of global publicity for the movement. Popular culture and academic literature alike show a fascination with the LTTE female fighter, invariably imagined as a suicide bomber, a sensationalised and sexualised 'Tamil Tigress' with her cyanide pendant dangling from her neck (Bloom 2005). The emergence of the LTTE female fighter as a multivalent figure in the war in Lanka pivots on the pervasive, if not always spoken, possibility of rape. Although Ambika Satkunanathan argues that 'The rape of women cadres…is never mentioned in LTTE literature or propaganda because it would have directly challenged the LTTE's rhetoric that militarisation leads to empowerment and enables a woman to protect herself' (2012), it is also the case that the unspoken prospect of rape defines the suicide bomber, throwing into sharp relief both her sexual vulnerability and her ultimate inviolability, as guaranteed by her talisman, the cyanide capsule. Sumathy points out that the female fighter functions within both mythic and sociopolitical economies of meaning: her emergence testifies to the crisis of the gendered institutions of dowry and property inheritance in

DOI: 10.1057/9781137444646.0011

a society convulsed by war and militarism as it simultaneously draws on traditional models of female chastity: 'What exactly does it mean when the virgin woman is married off to death, carrying around her neck the cyanide capsule like the *Tali* (sacred thread worn around the neck—a symbol of marital status for the woman) and is seen as married to the cause and its leader?' (2004, 135). But if being 'married off to death', and to the leader/cause, is one answer to the question of a surplus of marriage-able women in a time of war, it is also the answer to the question of rape, an answer that draws on a store of mytho-historical precedents in which the threat or act of rape is met with an act of self-annihilation.

The figure of the LTTE female cadre/suicide bomber combines in herself the characteristics of survivor and avenger: the raped woman who embodies the threat of retribution for the atrocities committed against her in the past, and who has the potential to escape the prospect of torture-rapes in the future, through the act of suicide bombing. As Maunaguru and others point out, 'there are multiple layers of meaning embodied in that mode of killing' (1995, 171). The avenging figure of the raped woman is shadowed by the figure of the woman rendered impure or polluted by rape: 'The woman killing her oppressor using her polluted body as a weapon symbolically performs two functions': avenging a crime that is understood as a violation of the homeland, and purification of a female body that has been rendered impure by rape (Maunaguru 1995, 170–71; Sumathy 2004, 142–3).

Dhanu, the LTTE fighter who became notorious for assassinating Indian Prime Minister Rajiv Gandhi by activating her suicide vest as she reached up to garland him at an election rally, had been, it was reported, raped by an Indian soldier. Later accounts suggested that it was not Dhanu herself, but her mother, who was raped by a member of the Indian Peace Keeping Force during battles with the LTTE in Jaffna in 1987–9. Another notorious bombing in 2006 was said to have been carried out by an LTTE fighter who became pregnant as a result of rape by the Lankan military (de Mel 2007, 209). A short story by V.V. Ganeshananthan, 'Hippocrates', alludes to this incident through the character of a pregnant suicide bomber who was herself the victim of mass violence in the form of a gang rape (2009). This persistent asso-ciation between rape and suicide bombing is one that circumscribes the agency of the female fighter within an economy of victim and avenger.

In the economy of suicide bombing, Gayatri Spivak asserts, 'there is no recoding of the gender struggle' (2004, 97). Spivak goes on to distinguish

DOI: 10.1057/9781137444646.0011

the actions of the female suicide bomber from the act at the centre of her most famous essay: 'Bhubaneswari Bhaduri, the subaltern in "Can the Subaltern Speak?" was a woman who used her gendered body to inscribe an unheard message; the bomber who died with Rajiv Gandhi, also a woman, did not' (ibid.). Tasked with carrying out an assassination in the Indian independence struggle, Bhubaneswari Bhaduri chose to take her own life instead, but waited until her menstruating body could speak her chastity, ensuring that the motivation for her suicide could not be construed as sexual transgression (Spivak 1998, 2004). The 'unheard message' of Buhaneswari's menstruating body, her refusal to kill, however, cannot be separated from a context in which ideologies of female chastity exert an inexorable hold, and in which female desire/sexuality and death are inextricably entwined. In this sense, 'Bhubaneswari', Spivak's exemplary figure of the subaltern, and 'Dhanu', the LTTE suicide bomber, signify not as opposites, but as gendered subjects both ensnared in a heteropatriarchal logic that leads surely to their deaths.

Economies of entrapment

Enmeshed in an economy of gendered nationalism, heteropatriachy and death, the LTTE female fighter/ suicide bomber has been understood as a figure of 'ambiguous empowerment' (de Mel 2007, 194; Coomaraswamy 1997), a warrior woman and 'armed virgin' who embodies both traditional masculine and feminine attributes: heroic self-sacrifice, martial virtue, revolutionary dedication. In Jasbir Puar's terms, the suicide bomber is one who queers and recombines disparate elements, as she confounds categories and orders of being (2007, 216–7). Focusing on spatial, rather than gendered, limits, Robert Williams, too, codes the suicide bomber as one who breaks through boundaries, to reveal that borders 'are not simply given in the order of things'. In the act of breaking through the seemingly self-enclosed and unimpregnable spaces of the nation and the homeland, 'the conceptual, ideological fiction of boundaries is destroyed or else vitiated' (2003, 283–4). In a similar vein, Achille Mbembe writes of the death of the suicide bomber in the Palestinian context as one that 'necessitates resolving the question of distance' between self and enemy through a death that 'goes hand in hand with the other':

DOI: 10.1057/9781137444646.0011

The candidate for martyrdom transforms his or her body into a mask that hides the soon-to-be detonated weapon. Thus concealed, it forms part of the body. It is so intimately part of the body that at the time of detonation it annihilates the body of its bearer, who carries with it the bodies of others when it does not reduce them to pieces

...In this instance, my death goes hand in hand with the death of the other...To detonate the bomb necessitates resolving the question of distance, through the work of proximity and concealment. How are we to interpret this manner of spilling blood in which death is not simply that which is my own, but always goes hand in hand with the death of the other? (2003, 36–7)

The bomber's corporeality, Mbembe points out, becomes a weapon, 'not in a metaphoric sense, but in a truly ballistic sense' (ibid.). Citing Mbembe in 2007, before the scenes at Mullivaikkal, I suggested that in Lanka, as in Palestine, the suicide bomber breaks apart geographies of entrapment and separation. Invested with seemingly supernatural powers, she penetrates unnoticed into the heart of enemy territory, clothed in unremarkability and dynamite. Weaving across minefields, edging through cracks in the border, or meticulously altering the function of everyday objects, metamorphosing identities and transmogrifying bodies, she annihilates distances between exception and every day, here and there, self and other (Perera 2007). These possibilities are extended in Puar's reflections on the suicide bombers as queer assemblages in the context of 9/11:

The spatial collapse of sides is due to the queer temporal interruption of the suicide bomber, projectiles spewing every which way. As a queer assemblage...race and sexuality are denaturalized through the impermanence, the transience of the suicide bomber...This dissolution of self into others/s and others/s into self not only effaces the absolute mark of self and other/s in the war on terror, but produces a systemic challenge to the entire order of Manichean rationality that organises the rubric of good versus evil. (2007, 218)

Still, the 'temporal and spatial re-orderings that the body iterates as it is machined together and explodes, cannot be other than transitory...The assemblage is momentary, fleeting even, and gives way to normative identity markers even in the midst of its newly becoming state' (ibid., 220). In its wake, spatial, racial and national identity markers are violently reasserted, as are the demarcations that separate good and evil, reason and unreason, homeland and frontier, self and other.

DOI: 10.1057/9781137444646.0011

The limits of horror

The torture-rape and mutilation of dead LTTE women by military and state forces both enacted the triumphalist supremacy of the conquering soldier over the body of the conquered and, at another level, forestalled the possibility of retribution by killing and mutilating the potential avenger—in some instances, by literally driving a stake or other lethal object through her body. As an iteration of conquest, the rape of the dead and the living, the penetration and mutilation of enemy bodies, Franco suggests, acts to render the other abject, so much waste matter, as it brutally asserts the raping self as powerful and whole.

In the aftermath of the horrific torture-rapes in the No Fire Zone during and after 2009, the documented atrocities that still continue in some places and that continue to haunt and torment, how are the stories of the LTTE's female cadres to be told and understood? Laleh Khalili's insightful study of the commemorative practices of Palestinian liberation observes that the meanings of nationalist symbols and iconographies do not remain stable, but are subject to fluctuate and adapt under conditions of displacement and deterritorialisation, as the nature of the conflict changes. At the same time, they are reshaped by the requirements and agendas of supranational institutions, global media and transnational donors, such as NGOs (2007, 2–3). Khalili traces the interplay of the heroic and tragic narratives through the various phases of Palestinian displacement: 'When nationalist militancy shaped the contours of Palestinian life in Lebanon, heroic narratives predominated', with the camps acting as the centre of Palestinian liberation activities between 1969 and 1982 (ibid., 111). In the period following the Oslo accord, this centre shifted to the Occupied Palestinian Territories, and the narratives of Palestinians in Lebanese camps were cast predominantly in a tragic mode ('the trauma drama') that was far more appealing to international audiences and donors (ibid., 33).

In the case of a defeated militant movement, such as that of the LTTE, the meanings of cultural icons and key events are subject to greater fluctuation and resignification. Even more critical are the relations among the movement's dispersed followers and survivors to the lost, the dead, tortured and disappeared. Chapter 4 discussed the ways in which a call for accountability, buttressed by the UN and international agencies, shapes the reporting of the last days of the war and the framing of the dead in ways that elide the responsibility of certain actors. Similarly, accounts

DOI: 10.1057/9781137444646.0011

of the torture-rapes of the LTTE's female fighters also are increasingly cast in the mode of the 'trauma drama', with the survivors as walking wounded called upon to testify repeatedly under the terms established by global media and international bodies. The Global Summit to End Sexual Violence in Conflict held in London in 2014, under the patronage of UK Foreign Secretary William Hague and global superstar Angelina Jolie, was a case in point of the staging of the trauma drama as a million dollar extravaganza.

In the context of the various mechanisms of transitional justice put in place in 'post-conflict' or transitional societies, Allen Feldman compares forms of biographical witnessing and testimony that are solicited by contemporary tribunals to the forms of testimony called forth in aboli-tionist circles in the lead-up to the US Civil War, in which the baring of the slave's scarred and wounded body, displaying the whip marks on her back, was a necessary testimony to the incontrovertible truth of the inhumanity of the slave-system. Feldman suggests that the symbolic and literal uncovering of the subject of atrocity repeats this movement of truth-recovery:

> in these earlier theaters of memory and regimes of truth, we can recognize the contemporary process of recovering an archive of human rights violations from postcolonial peripheries, from closed societies, and from subjugated, vertically positioned social strata and their respective subaltern groups. (2004, 190)

The recovery enacts a movement of exposure and the descent into dark places: 'Trauma as buried truth is located in the body... and in alien geography, and must be brought up to the surface in modes of exposure and display, including pain and language' (ibid.). These remarks are instantly applicable to the reports of torture-rape in the Lankan conflict. The HRW report previously cited is a literal example, displaying on its cover a bare-backed subject exposing the brand marks he had received during torture by the Lankan army.

The importance of reports such as those by HRW in documenting and publicising instances of atrocity cannot be overestimated—indeed I have relied on them extensively throughout this study. Yet, as Feldman and others suggest, to bare the truth of the tortured body before the tribunals and publics of international law is to reinstall it within a conceptual and political framework of intelligibility and representability that yet remains inadequate to the forms of horrific violence and agonal sovereignty to which it has been subjected. The institutional conditions in which these

DOI: 10.1057/9781137444646.0011

frameworks operate, such as transitional justice and reparations, floun-
der in the face of the horrors they attempt to excavate and adjudicate.

Disjointed unfolding

'Confronted with horrifying sights, facts, descriptions, or sentiments that
are beyond thought', Debrix and Barder write, the temptation is to 'rally
around the mark of the human, around human life, or around the idea
of human integrity or identity' (2012, 130). Against the limits of the call
for international accountability, the task of responding to the violence of
agonal sovereignty, Debrix and Barder suggest, calls for other tactics, a
reflection of its horrific excesses: an ethic that aspires, not to recover or
remake the bodies and lives unmade by an excess of sovereign violence,
but a practice they describe as 'inventorying the scattered', to offer 'openness as a counterpoint to horror's gaping hole or wound' (ibid., 130). One
such attempt is Sumathy's long essay, 'A Spoonful of Sugar: The Quest
for Survival and Justice in the Violence of Gender and the Violence of
Sex in the Politics of the Ethnic Conflict in Sri Lanka'. The essay weaves
together a collaborative telling, a dialectics of voices with testimony,
poetry and theory, in an attempt to mark 'something that we cannot
quite grasp within the discursivity provided by the academic-activist
rhetoric of violation, human rights, mass murder and sexual violence'.
In its discontinuities and transpositions, its barrage of stories and blurring and merging of voices, the essay aims to 'reconceptualise justice as
a process' and 'the only means through which we can chart a route for
women's narratives' (forthcoming).

Faced with the pyres on the banks of the Nanthikadal lagoon, the
grainy images on trophy cell phone videos, the pile of bloodless bodies
over which the camera pans, I turn to Debrix and Barder's meditation
on the politico-ethical implications of narrating the unspeakable. As it
'cannot wish to 'return to the violence that reduces the human to ashes to
be dispersed by the wind', they put forward an ethics of inventorying the
scattered that works through 'being dispersed, by tracking some body
parts, bits of flesh, ashes and other human and non-human remains'.
As a practice of telling, this is an ethics that attempts 'a disjointed
unfolding'; one that does not claim to be 'thorough, exhaustive, logical,
linear, or even constructive'. It distinguishes itself from modes such as
testimony or witness-bearing, proposing not resolution but 'openness

DOI: 10.1057/9781137444646.0011

as a counterpoint to horror's gaping hole or wound'. 'It resists the drive to reconstruct the body of life, even a body beyond the body, or a life beyond life' but 'enables an opening, a space to rethink relations between what is alive and what is not, and perhaps, just as crucially, between what may be alive or always subject to death'. At best, this is an ethics that 'offers a few terms, a few concepts, a few signposts along the way to draw our attention to that which has been pulverized…It resists the all too common impulse to closure in the face of horror' (2012, 130).

***

> Why am I approached
> by this kind of poem
> and this terrible night?
> in the end after all
> my words fall flat.
> am I supposed now to write an ode
> on the children's battleground?

Deebachelvan's poem, 'Let's move on again' is dedicated to a younger sister, Vengani, taken by the LTTE towards the end of the war:

> at an age when you knew nothing
> you were given a war
> the gun given into your hand
> is ripening your raw heart
> the remaining ground gives itself up to the enemy.
> …
> at this time we have no city either
> we have no life.
> we who have nothing
> are ourselves absent
> still we need you
> to eat with us the little bit of half-cooked rice
> and boiled lentils
> come quickly
> let's move on again, to yet another place.

(Kannan et al. 2014, 184–5)

DOI: 10.1057/9781137444646.0011

Conclusion—'From What Has Happened to What Will Come'

Abstract: *The conclusion considers the possibilities for reconciliation in the light of V.V. Ganeshananthan's poem, 'We regret to inform you'.*

Keywords: percepticide; reconciliation; V.V. Ganeshananthan

Perera, Suvendrini. *Survival Media: The Politics and Poetics of Mobility and the War in Sri Lanka.* New York: Palgrave Macmillan, 2016. DOI: 10.1057/9781137444646.0012.

DOI: 10.1057/9781137444646.0012

V.V. Ganeshananthan's beautiful poem, 'We regret to inform you', appeared in an anthology to commemorate the first anniversary of the war's ending. Precise, formal and laceratingly polite, the narrator offers a lucid rejection of the processes of reconciliation and condolence that have become standard in 'post-conflict' and 'transitional justice' scenarios:

> We regret to inform you that your condolences cannot be accepted at this time. At present, both our pain and our hope defy that word, which has been offered and denied us, which we need and do not need, and which in any case we cannot accept, because they (your condolences) will not reach from what has happened to what will come.
>
> We find the word *condolences* stunning in its insufficiency for past and future.
>
> In the rush to escape this bloodletting, which has been its own kind of war, our ears fell to the ground, and so we cannot now hear your condolences. To survive, we had to shut our eyes, with which we would have seen what was in yours. We closed our mouths against hunger and anger; we knew and did not know our families, friends, fellows, and leaders, who hunted us, ran with us, and died with us. (Ganeshananthan, 2010)

The poem recalls Diana Taylor's discussion of 'percepticide' in Argentina's dirty war, as one that 'blinds, maims and kills through the senses': 'What happens to the "witness" in a situation that forces people to participate in the production of denial? The passers-by, the neighbors, could not bear witness: they closed the door, shut the curtains, turned off the light' (1997, 124).

No less than the witness and the bystander, the subject and survivor of violence is caught in the violence that allows her to see only the 'given-to-be-seen', and to close her eyes to the 'given-to-be-denied' (1997).

Ganeshananthan's poem suggests that percepticide, as a paradoxical act in which subjects maim and deaden their own senses in order to preserve themselves from lethal violence from without, was the only course open to those who survived the war. Written five years after the end of the war, Rajan Hoole's *Palmyra Fallen* calls into account not only those immediate witnesses who shut their eyes, caught between the overweening supremacism of the state and the LTTE's blind opposition to it, but the wilful blindness of diasporic and expatriate intellectuals: 'even as the cause became untenable...they argued for shutting one's eyes and conscience and sticking with it, whatever the cost to others (2015, 144).

DOI: 10.1057/9781137444646.0012

At the conclusion of the war, in the variable light of transitional justice, subjects who shut their eyes, who knew and did not know, themselves become visible anew as survivors. Again and again, Hoole, whose organisation, University Teachers for Human Rights (Jaffna) rigorously documented the violence on all sides in the war, calls for a critical understanding of their own complicity in the rise of the LTTE by 'mainstream Tamil society' in Lanka and elsewhere: 'A wronged minority is duty bound to appeal to international laws and covenants. Still, when it does so with its house full of murder and deceit, it may offer the world an unsolvable dilemma. Now that the LTTE is gone, that dilemma becomes more tractable' (ibid., 158).

In the absence of such a comprehensive accounting, will Ganeshananthan's survivors who shut their ears, eyes and mouths in 'the rush to escape this bloodletting' remain silent, insensate, impervious? Here is no garrulous survivor or compliant trauma subject, ready to bare its scars in the service of reconciliation, but one which remains mute, obdurate, self-enclosed. It speaks only through its act of refusal, conveying the impossibility of that which is being asked of it in the project of reconstruction: 'We faced ourselves from all sides. Some of us lived. We are still here. We regret to inform you that your condolences cannot be accepted at this time' (Ganeshananthan, 2010).

What languages, other than those of silence, are adequate to 'reach from what has happened to what will come'? Against the carefully delimited solicitations of truth commissions and human rights tribunals, how to articulate the unspeakable shadows that attend their claims to let in the light? Hoole argues that letting in the light calls for an accounting that begins at home. I read Ganeshananthan's poem itself as the beginning of such an accounting, an acknowledgement of the relations in which the survivor and the lost, the disappeared and living, are bound up in one another.

Even in the extremity of the survivors' grief and pain, the proffered condolences, it must be noted, are not completely rejected: it is acknowledged that they are something 'we need and do not need'. The poem carries the slightest hint of a future when things might be different: 'Your condolences cannot be accepted' *at this time* leaves open the possibility that at another time, the eyes, mouths and ears that have been sealed shut by this bloodletting, rendered insensate by the horrors of what they endured, will be unblocked: able, once more, to see, hear and speak. The gesture towards a time that is as yet unimaginable holds

DOI: 10.1057/9781137444646.0012

out the possibility of a temporality to come in which condolences and acts of reaching out themselves are not clearly delineated and finite acts, but a sequence that is incremental, collaborative, iterative. In the future that is now outside imagining, is it conceivable that condolences may be offered and accepted from within as well as without? The question must remain open.

DOI: 10.1057/9781137444646.0012

Afterword

Perera, Suvendrini. *Survival Media: The Politics and Poetics of Mobility and the War in Sri Lanka*. New York: Palgrave Macmillan, 2016. DOI: 10.1057/9781137444646.0013.

▶

DOI: 10.1057/9781137444646.0013

In his acceptance speech upon being awarded the Nobel Prize in literature, Derek Walcott reflects that 'For every poet it is always morning in
the world. History a forgotten, insomniac night; History and elemental
awe are always our early beginning, because the fate of poetry is to fall
in love with the world, in spite of History.'[1] Suvendrini Perera takes us
on a journey through that night, where the world maps we traverse are
kept awake by history's challenge. The poetry birthed in the interstices
of those challenges becomes our co-traveller in relation to a dawn that
is ever receding on one side, and, on the other, ever present as an out of
reach beacon lighting our path. This book is a prolonged meditation on
the politics of mobility through a tracing of the geography of inequality
through poems and passports, refugees and international civil servants,
law and war.

Perera says early on that hers is not a project anchored in abiding by
Sri Lanka (invoking Qadri Ismail's formulation of the commitments that
drive his political and intellectual projects). In contrast, Perera describes
her project as one with no fixed abode Yet this does not mean it is root-
less; rather, I would argue that Perera's project abides by the *passage*. With
poetic prose and keen analysis, the book shows us that the refugee and
migrant are not only mobile subjects; tracing their fraught passage also
complicates, disorients and troubles the question of the subject itself.
This tracing, like the cartographer's palimpsestic making of new maps,
layered over older ones, calls attention to the historical contingency
and political instability of subjectivity as it is enriched, dislocated and
hybridised by the chronotope of other subjectivities. Like precarious
island-hopping along that passage, the subject struggles for shore, then
slips from view, only to remerge: each time constituted by, and struggling
with, trajectories of power and knowledge that are both new and not.
For instance, tracing the 'ethnoracial politics of present-day Lanka' takes
Perera places—from the 'disastrous conjoining of two broad systems of
differentiation, indigenous and colonial' in nineteenth- and twentieth-
century colonial Sri Lanka, to the biopolitical governance technologies of
post-colonial Sri Lanka in the 1970s, to refugee laws and policies forged
in the aftermath of Europe's twentieth-century wars that then shaped
Britain's reception of Tamil refugees, to the sense of 'belonging' imparted
to a young Tamil girl in South London by hip-hop shaped in the crucible
of urban America's racial and class wars. Perera's abiding political and
intellectual commitment to a granular survey of each of these places and
their creolised genealogies profoundly unmoors the subject.

DOI: 10.1057/9781137444646.0013

This is a book that works from the grains of sand scattered across different landscapes to speak of a world on the move. These are not only geographic landscapes, but also disciplinary ones—from fiction and theater, to political sociology and history. The book offers a compass to the continuities and discontinuities of power and knowledge that link and differentiate the shores of Mullaitivu in northeastern Sri Lanka and Geraldton, in Western Australia—amongst other shores in those countries and elsewhere—from Palestine and Israel, to Guniea and Belgium. Indeed, it is a book that shows us that it is impossible to think geography without history, to think of roots without routes, to map mobility without mapping inequality, to think of today without our imaginary of the future.

Vasuki Nesiah
New York University
August 2015

Note

1   Derek Walcott (1992) *The Antilles: Fragments of Epic Memory: the Nobel Lecture.*

DOI: 10.1057/9781137444646.0013

Bibliography

Absolute Lyrics (n.d.) 'Galang – M.I.A.', accessed 25
    October 2012, absolutelyrics.com/lyrics/view/m.i.a./
    galang/.

Anderson, Jon Lee (2011) 'Death of the Tiger', *The New
    Yorker*, 17 January, accessed 3 March 2014. newyorker.
    com/magazine/2011/01/17/death-of-the-tiger/.

Anderson, Sean and Jennifer Ferng (2013) 'No Boat: The
    Architecture of Christmas Island' *Architectural Theory
    Review* 18.2: 212–226.

Appadurai, Arjun (1993) 'Number in the Colonial
    Imagination', in C.A. Breckenridge & P. van der Veer,
    eds. *Orientalism and the Postcolonial Predicament*
    (Philadelphia: University of Pennsylvania Press)
    314–39.

_____. (2003) 'Disjuncture and Difference in a Global
    Economy' in Jana Evans Braziel & Anita Mannur, eds.
    Theorizing Diaspora (London: Blackwell) 25–48.

Arasanayagam, Jean (2009) 'Rendition', *Sunday Times*
    (Sri Lanka) August 3 2008, accessed 20 January
    2010 http://www.sundaytimes.lk/080803/Plus/
    sundaytimesplus_01.html.

Arulpragasam, Mathangi Maya (2012) *M.I.A.* (New York:
    Rizzoli).

Auden, W.H. (1976) *Collected Poems*. Edited by
    E. Mendelson (London: Faber & Faber).

Australian (2007) 'Reaching for Dog Whistle and Stick',
    editorial, 2 August.

Balasingham, Adele Ann (1993) *Women Fighters of
    Liberation Tigers* (Jaffna: LTTE).

Balint, Ruth (2005) *Troubled Waters* (Sydney: Allen & Unwin).

Bastians, Dharisha (2015) 'In Gesture to Tamils, Sri Lanka Replaces Provincial Leader', *New York Times*, 15 January, http://www. nytimes.com/2015/01/16/world/asia/new-sri-lankan-leader-replaces-governor-of-tamil-stronghold.html?smprod=nytcore-ipad&smid=nytcore-ipad-share&_r=0.

Bavinck, Ben (2011) *Of Tamils and Tigers: A Journey Through Sri Lanka's War Years* (Colombo: Vijita Yapa and Rajini Thiranagama Memorial Committee).

Brager, Jenna (2015). 'Bodies of Water', *The New Inquiry*, May 12, http://thenewinquiry.com/essays/bodies-of-water/.

Beehner, Lionel (2010) 'What Sri Lanka Can Teach Us about COIN', *Small Wars Journal* 27.

Bloom, Mia (2005) *Dying to Kill: The Allure of Suicide Terror* (New York: Columbia University Press).

Bora, Papori (2010) 'Between the Human, the Citizen, and the Tribal', *International Feminist Journal of Politics* 12 (3–4): 341–60.

Brown, Jayna (2010) 'Buzz and Rumble Global Pop Music and Utopian Impulse' *Social Text* 102 (28.1): 125–46.

Brunero, Tim (2007) 'The Tim Offensive: Citizenship Tests'. YouTube video. Accessed 15 October 2007. youtube.com/watch?v=FKWFwsyyZb8/.

Bush, George W. (2001) 'Address to Joint Session of Congress', 20 September, georgewbush-whitehouse.archives.gov/news/releases/2001/09/20010920-8.html.

Chang, Jeff (2007) 'News from Nowhere', *The Nation*, 19 November, thenation.com/article/news-nowhere?page=0.

Cavarero, Adriana (2009) *Horrorism: Naming Contemporary Violence* (New York: Columbia University Press).

Channel 4 (UK) (2013) 'Fate of Tamil Propagandist: New Sri Lanka Evidence – Video', 31 October. Accessed 11 November 2014. channel4.com/news/fate-of-tamil-actress-chilling-new-evidence-from-sri-lanka/.

Christgau, Robert (2005) 'Burning Bright' *Village Voice*, 22 February. villagevoice.com/2005-02-22/music/burning-bright/.

Cochrane, L. (2010) 'Romain Gavras: Born Free Director Is No Stranger to Stress', *The Guardian*, 25 September.

Comaroff, Jean & John L. Comaroff (2006) *Law and Disorder in the Postcolony.* (Chicago: University of Chicago Press).

DOI: 10.1057/9781137444646.0014

Coomaraswamy, Radhika (1997) 'Tiger Women and the Question of Women's Emancipation', *Pravda* 4 (9): 8–10.

———— and Nimanthi Perera-Rajasingham (2009) 'Being Tamil in a Different Way', in R. Cheran, ed. *Pathways of Dissent: Tamil Nationalism in Sri Lanka* (New Delhi: Sage) 107–38.

CNN (2001) 'Prison Watchdog Slams Refugee Conditions'. *CNN*, edition. cnn.com/2001/WORLD/asiapcf/auspac/10/30/aust.refugees.disgrace/.

Daniel, E. Valentine & Yuvaraj Thangaraj (1995) 'Forms, Formations and Transformations of the Tamil Refugee', in E. Valentine Daniel & John Chr. Knudsen, eds. *Mistrusting Refugees* (Berkeley: University of California Press), 225–56.

Debrix, Francois & Alexander D. Barder (2012) *Beyond Biopolitics* (New York: Routledge).

Deleuze, Gilles & Felix Guattari (1980) *A Thousand Plateaus: Capitalism and Schizophrenia*. Translated and foreword by Brian Massumi. (Minneapolis: University of Minnesota Press).

De Mel, Niloufer (2001) *Women and the Nation's Narrative* (New Delhi: Kali for Women).

————. (2007) *Militarizing Sri Lanka* (New Delhi: Sage).

Derrida, Jacques (1993) *Spectres of Marx: The State of the Debt, the Work of Mourning, and the New International*. Translated by Peggy Kamuf. (New York: Routledge).

————. (2005) *Rogues*. Translated by Michael Naas. (Stanford: Stanford University Press).

DeVotta, Neil (2004) *Blowback: Linguistic Nationalism, Institutional Decay, and Ethnic Conflict in Sri Lanka* (Stanford: Stanford University Press).

D'Lo (2008) 'Beats, Rhythm, Life' in Ajay Nair & Murali Balaji, eds. *Desi Rap: Hip-Hop and South Asian America* (London: Lexington Books).

d'Souza, Radha (2012) 'A Fleeting Moment in Times of Cognitive Dissonance', Foreword to N. Malathy, *A Fleeting Moment in My Country* (Atlanta, GA: Clear Day Books).

Durham, Meenakshi Gigi (2009) 'M.I.A.: A Production Analysis of Musical Subversion' (Chicago: International Communication Association, Feminist Scholarship Division).

Dutta, Abhijit (2013) '22 years after Kunan and Poshpora, Rethinking Kashmir', *Kafila: Media, Politics, Dissent*, 23 February. Accessed 20 January 2014. http://kafila.org/2013/02/23/22-years- after-kunan-and-poshpora-rethinking-kashmir-abhijit-dutta/.

DOI: 10.1057/9781137444646.0014

Edmund Rice Centre (2004 & 2006) *Deported to Danger*, Vols 1 and 2. (Homebush: Edmund Rice Centre).

Eliot, T.S. (1971 [1920]) *The Complete Poems and Plays 1909–1950* (New York: Harcourt Brace & World Inc.).

Empire, Kitty (2005) 'Flash Forward', *The Observer*, 20 March, observer. guardian.co.uk/omm/story/0,,1438918,00.html.

Feldman, Allen (2004) 'Memory Theaters, Virtual Witnessing, and the Trauma-Aesthetic', *Biography* 27 (1): 163–202.

_____. (2006) 'On the Actuarial Gaze' *Cultural Studies* 19 (2): 203–26.

Fernandes, Sujatha (2011) *Close to the Edge: In Search of the Hip-Hop Generation* (New York: Random House).

Fitzpatrick, Stephen (2009) 'Finally, the Real Alex Steps Forward', *The Australian*, 9 November. theaustralian.com.au/news/finally-the-real-alex-steps-forward/story-e6frg6n6-1225795570337.

Foundas, Scott (2015) 'Cannes Film Review: *Dheepan*', *Variety*, 21 May. http://variety.com/2015/film/festivals/dheepan-film-review-cannes-1201502383/.

Franco, Jean (2013) *Cruel Modernity* (Durham: Duke University Press).

Frere-Jones, Sasha (2004) 'Bingo in Swansea', *New Yorker*, 22 November. newyorker.com/ archive/2004/11/22/041122crmu_music#ixzz1OeGqbkav.

_____. (2012) 'M.I.A. Shouldn't Have Apologized', *New Yorker*, 6 February. newyorker.com/online/blogs/culture/2012/02/im-sorry-mia-ap.

Galligan, Brian & John Chesterman (1999) 'Australia's Citizenship Void', in *Globalization and Citizenship in the Asia-Pacific*, A. Davidson & K. Weekley, eds. (Basingstoke: Macmillan) 73–86.

Ganeshananthan, V.V. (2008) *Love Marriage* (New York: Random House).

_____. (2010) 'We Regret To Inform You That Your Condolences Cannot Be Accepted at This Time' in *End of War in Sri Lanka: Reflections and Challenges*, accessed 15 June 2010, groundviews. org/2010/05/20/we-regret-to-inform-you-that-your-condolences-cannot-be-accepted-at-this-time/.

_____. (2010) 'Hippocrates' *Granta* 109http://granta.com/hippocrates/.

Getler, M. 2009, 'Rapping about genocide', *PBS Ombudsman*, 12 February. pbs.org/ombudsman/2009/02/rapping_about_genocide_1. htm/, viewed 25 October 2012.

Ghosh, Amitav (2003) 'The Greatest Sorrow: Times of Joy Recalled in Wretchedness', *Kenyon Review*, Summer/Fall. http://www.kenyonreview. org/journal/summerfall-2003/selections/the-greatest-sorrow/.

DOI: 10.1057/9781137444646.0014

Grattan, M. & Allard, T. (2009) 'Not Sorry: PM Unmoved by Pleas", *Age*, 16 October. http://www.theage.com.au/national/not-sorry-pm-unmoved-by-pleas-20091015-gz5y.html.

Groundviews (2012) 'The End of the War in Sri Lanka Captured for Posterity by Google Earth', *Groundviews*. http://groundviews. org/2012/09/12/the-end-of-war-in-sri-lanka-captured-for-posterity-by-google-earth/.

Hall, Stuart (2012) 'Avtar Brah's Cartographies: Moment, Method, Meaning', *Feminist Review* 100: 27–38.

Harrison, Francis (2012) *Still Counting the Dead* (London: Portobello Books).

Hartmann, Florence & Ed Vulliamy (2015) 'How Britain and the U.S. Decided to Abandon Srebrenica to Its Fate', *Guardian*, July 5. http:// www.theguardian.com/world/2015/jul/04/how-britain-and-us-abandoned-srebrenica-massacre-1995.

Haviland, Charles de (2011) 'Sri Lanka to Hold Militancy Summit', *BBC*, 24 May, accessed 7 November 2014. bbc.co.uk/news/world-south-asia-13518949/.

Hernandez, Vittorio (2012) 'Navy Burns Asylum Boats', *The Advertiser*, 20 July. ibtimes.com/articles/365031/20120720/navy-burns-asylum-boats.htm#.U1ivWlWSzE0.

Hirschberg, Lynn (2010) 'M.I.A's Agitprop Pop', *New York Times*, 25 May. nytimes.com/2010/05/30/magazine/30mia-t. html?src=tp&pagewanted=2.

Hoole, Rajan, D. Somasundaram, K. Sritharan & R. Thiranagama (1990) *The Broken Palmyrah* (Claremont, California: The Sri Lanka Studies Institute).

Hoole, Rajan (2015) *Palmyra Fallen From Rajini to War's End* (Jaffna: University Teachers for Human Rights [Jaffna]).

Hulme, Peter (2004) 'Cast Away', in *Sea Changes: Historicizing the Ocean*, B. Klein & G. Mackenthun, eds., (London: Routledge) 187–97.

———. (2005) 'Beyond the Straits: Postcolonial Allegories of the Globe', in *Postcolonial Studies and Beyond*, A. Loomba, S. Kaul, M. Bunzl, A. Burton, & J. Esty, eds. (Durham: Duke University Press) 41–61.

Human Rights Watch [HRW] (2009) 'Sri Lanka: UN Rights Council Fails Victims', *HRW*, 27 May. hrw.org/news/2009/05/27/sri-lanka-un-rights-council-fails-victims.

———. (2013) *'We Will Teach You a Lesson': Sexual Violence against Tamils by Sri Lankan Security Forces* (New York: Human Rights

DOI: 10.1057/9781137444646.0014

Watch), accessed 3 January 2014. hrw.org/sites/default/files/reports/
srilanka0213webwcover_0.pdf/.

Hyndman, Jennifer & Malathi de Alwis (2005) 'Performing the
Pass: Conflict, Mobility and Displacement in Sri Lanka', in *Asian
Migrations: Sojourning, Displacement, Homecoming and Other Travels*,
B.P. Lorente, N. Piper, Shen Sui-Hua & Brenda Yeoh, eds. (Singapore:
Asian Research Institute) 25–49.

International Crimes Evidence Project [ICEP] (2014) *Island of Impunity*
(Sydney: Public Interest Advocacy Centre).

International Crisis Group [ICG] (2010) 'War Crimes in Sri Lanka', *Asia
Report* 191, 19.

_____. (2011) 'Sri Lanka: Women's Insecurity in the North and East',
Asia Report, 20 December, 217.

Ismail, Qadri (2005) *Abiding by Sri Lanka* (Minneapolis: University of
Minnesota Press).

Jayawardena, Kumari (1983) 'Class and Ethnic Consciousness Part 2',
Lanka Guardian 6 (6): 17–20.

Jazeel, Tariq (2009) 'Reading the Geography of Sri Lankan Island-ness:
Colonial Repetitions, Postcolonial Possibilities', *Contemporary South
Asia* 17 (4): 399–414.

Jeganathan, Pradeep (2002) 'Walking Through Violence: "Everyday Life"
and Anthropology', in *Everyday Life in South Asia*, Diane P. Mines &
Sarah Lamb, eds. (Bloomington: Indiana University Press) 357–65.

Jeyaraj, D.B.S. (2014) 'Shooting Incident at Tharmapuram: Is There a
Real LTTE Resurgence in the North?' *DBSJeyaraj.com*, 27 March,
accessed 28 March 2014. dbsjeyaraj.com/dbsj/archives/28949/.

Joseph, May (1999) *Nomadic Identities: The Performance of Citizenship*
(Minneapolis: Minnesota University Press).

Kadirgamar, Ahilan (2010) 'Classes, States and the Politics of the Tamil
Diaspora', *Economic & Political Weekly* xlv (31): 23–6.

Kannan M., Rebecca Whittington, D. Senthil Babu, David C. Buck
(2014) *Time Will Write a Song for You: Contemporary Tamil Writing from
Sri Lanka* (Delhi: Penguin India).

Kearney, S. (2009) ' "We'd Rather Die Than Go Ashore Here': Sri Lankan
Asylum-seekers' *Australian*, 28 October, accessed 30 October 2012.
theaustralian.com.au/news/world/wedrather-die-than-go-ashore-
here-srilankan-asylumseekers/storye6frg6so-1225791914062/.

Kelley, Robin D.H. (1997) *Yo' Mama's Disfunktional: Fighting the Culture
Wars in Urban America* (Boston: Beacon).

DOI: 10.1057/9781137444646.0014

Khalili, Laleh (2007) *Heroes and Martyrs of Palestine: The Politics of National Liberation* (Cambridge: Cambridge University Press).

Kilcullen, David (2011) 'Overview of Terrorism', *Business Today*, accessed 2 November 2012. businesstoday.lk/article.php?article=3483#sthash. XgEJANfS.dpuf/.

Kishawi, Sami (2014) 'Controversial, Illegal, and Documented: Israeli Military Strategies in Gaza', *Mondo Weiss*, 25 July, accessed 30 July 2014. mondoweiss.net/2014/07/controversial-documented-strategies#sthash.ezuDAMRx.dpuf/.

Kleinfeld, Margo (2005) 'Destabilizing the Identity – Territory Nexus: Rights-based Discourse in Sri Lanka's New Political Geography', *GeoJournal* 64: 287–95.

Krishna, Sankaran (1999) *Postcolonial Insecurities: India, Sri Lanka, and the Question of Nationhood* (Minneapolis: University of Minnesota Press).

Kundnani, Arun (2007) *The End of Tolerance: Racism in 21st Century Britain* (London: Pluto Press).

Lee, Matthew Russell (2009) 'Sri Lanka Damage Satellite Photos Withheld by UNITAR, IOM Staff Detained', *Inner City Press*, 29 April. http://www.innercitypress.com/iom1unitar042909.html.

Lorde, Audre (1984) *Sister Outsider* (New York: Crossing Press).

Lowe, Lisa (1996) *Immigrant Acts: On Asian American Cultural Politics* (Durham: Duke University Press).

MacIntyre, Ernest (1990) *Rasanayagam's Last Riot* (Sydney: Wordlink).

Mackey, Robert (2009) 'Outside Sri Lanka, Tamil Diaspora Not Ready to Surrender', *New York Times*, 18 May. thelede.blogs.nytimes.com/2009/05/18/outside-sri-lanka-tamil-diaspora-not-ready-to-surrender/?_r=0.

Malathy, N. (2012) *A Fleeting Moment in My Country* (Atlanta: Clear Day Books).

Manikkalingam, Ram (1995) *Tigerism and Other Essays* (Colombo: Ethnic Studies Group).

Marga Institute (2014) *The Third Narrative* (Colombo: Marga Institute)

Maunaguru, Sitralega (1995) 'Gendering Tamil Nationalism: The Construction of "Woman" in Projects of Protest and Control', in *Unmaking the Nation: The Politics of Identity and History in Modern Sri Lanka*, Pradeep Jeganathan & Qadri Ismail, eds. (Colombo: Social Scientists' Association) 158–75.

Mbembe, Achille (2003) 'Necropolitics', translated by L. Meintjes, *Public Culture* 15 (1): 11–40.

DOI: 10.1057/9781137444646.0014

Ministry of Defence, Sri Lanka (2010) 'Forces Maintained Zero Civilian Casualty Rate at All Times', Media Release 30 December, accessed 30 July 2014. defence.lk/new.asp?fname=20100912_01/.

———. (2011) ' "Only We Can Solve Our Own Problems, and None Other" – President', Presidential Address, 28 May, accessed 30 July 2014. defence.lk/new.asp?fname=20110527_07/

Mohan, Rohini (2014) *Seasons of Trouble* (London: Verso).

Ngai, Mae (2003) *Impossible Subjects: Illegal Aliens and the Making of Modern America* (Princeton: Princeton University Press).

Neruda, Pablo (1950) 'Los Dictadores', http://famouspoetsandpoems. com/poets/pablo_neruda/poems/15737.

Office of the High Commissioner for Human Rights (OHCHR) (2014) 'Human Rights Council Adopts a Resolution on Reconciliation, Accountability and Human Rights in Sri Lanka', Media Release, 27 March, accessed 30 July 2014. ohchr.org/EN/NewsEvents/Pages/ DisplayNews.aspx?NewsID=14447&LangID=E#sthash.s9TJvEzq.dpuf.

Ong, Aihwa (2003) 'Cultural Citizenship as Subject Making: Immigrants Negotiate Racial and Cultural Boundaries in the United States', in *Race, Identity and Citizenship*, R. D. Torres, L. F. Miron & J. X. Inda, eds. (Malden: Blackwell) 262–93.

Orlov, Piotr (2005) 'Interview with M.I.A.', *Arthur* 16 May. arthurmag. com/2007/02/11/interview-with-mia-from-arthur-magazine/.

Orr, Aleisha (2013) 'Asylum Seeker Boat in Geraldton', *WA Today*, 9 April, accessed 13 September 2014. watoday.com.au/wa-news/ asylum-seeker-boat-in-geraldton-20130409-2hjos.html/.

Osborne, Charles (1980) *W.H. Auden, The Life of a Poet* (London: Eyre Methuen).

Perera, Suvendrini (2001) 'A Chaos of Stories', Program Notes, Theatre of Migration Dir. Ernest MacIntyre.

———. (2002) 'A Line in the Sea', *Race & Class* 44 (2): 23–39.

———. (2006) 'They Give Evidence': Bodies, Borders and the Disappeared', *Social Identities* 12 (6): 637–56.

———. (2007) 'Our Patch: Domains of Whiteness, Geographies of Lack and Australia's New Politics of Space in the War on Terror', in *Our Patch: Australian Sovereignty Post-2001*, S. Perera, ed. (Perth: Network Books) 119–46.

———. (2009) *Australia and the Insular Imagination: Beaches, Borders, Boats and Bodies* (New York: Palgrave-Macmillan).

DOI: 10.1057/9781137444646.0014

_____. (2014a) 'Dead Exposures: Trophy Bodies and Violent Visibilities of the Nonhuman', *Borderlands* 13 (1).

_____. (2014b) 'Viewing Violence in a Far Country: Abu Ghraib and Terror's New Performativities', in *At the Limits of Justice: Women of Color on Terror*, Suvendrini Perera & Sherene Razack, eds. (Toronto: University of Toronto Press) 455–71.

Puar, Jasbir (2007) *Terrorist Assemblages: Homonationalism in Queer Times* (Durham: Duke University Press).

Pugliese, Joseph (2001) 'Penal Asylum: Refugees, Ethics, Hospitality', *Borderlands*, 1 (1). borderlands.net.au/vol1no1_2002/pugliese.html.

_____. (2005) 'The Incommensurability of Law to Justice: Refugees and Australia's Temporary Protection Visa', *Law and Literature* 16 (3): 285–311.

_____. (2011) 'Civil Modalities of Refugee Trauma, Death and Necrological Transport' In *Living Through Terror*, Suvendrini Perera and Antonio Traverso, eds. (Abingdon: Routledge) 142–58.

_____. (2013) *State Violence and the Execution of Law* (New York: Routledge).

Rajapaksa, Mahinda (2009) 'President's Speech to Parliament on the Defeat of LTTE', *SATP*, 19 May. satp.org/satporgtp/countries/shrilanka/document/papers/president_speech_parliament_defeatofLTTE.htm.

Ratner, Steven R. (2012) 'Accountability and the Sri Lankan Civil War', *American Journal of International Law* 106 (4): 795–808.

Reuters News Agency (2009) 'Tamil Tigers Say War at "Bitter End"', 17 May. reuters.com/article/worldNews/idUSTRE54G0Q920090517.

Reynolds, Henry (2007) 'Part of a Continent for Something Less Than a Nation? The Limits of Australian Sovereignty', In *Our Patch: Enacting Australian Sovereignty Post-2001*, S. Perera, ed. (Perth: Network Books) 61–70.

Sandoval, Chela (2000) *Methodology of the Oppressed* (Minneapolis: Minnesota University Press).

Sarvananthan, Muttukrishna (2009) 'M.I.A. and the Bogey of Genocide in Sri Lanka', *Sunday Leader*, 1 March. thesundayleader.lk/20090301/Issues-1.htm.

Satkunananthan, Ambika (2012) 'Whose Nation? Power, Agency, Gender and Tamil Nationalism' in *The Sri Lankan Republic at 40: Reflections on Constitutional History, Theory and Practice*, Asanga Welikala, ed. (Colombo: Centre for Policy Alternatives) 613–40.

DOI: 10.1057/9781137444646.0014

Sawyer, Miranda (2010) 'MIA: "I'm Here for the People"'. *The Observer*, 13 June. guardian.co.uk/music/2010/jun/13/mia-feature-miranda-sawyer.

Shapiro, Peter (2005) 'Talking about Her Revolution', *The Times*, 17 June, thetimes.co.uk/tto/arts/article2400924.ece.

Shanaathanan, T. (2011) *The Incomplete Thombu* (n.p.: Raking Leaves).

Shobasakthi (2012) 'Warscapes in Conversation with Shobasakthi', translated by Anushya Ramaswamy. warscapes.com/conversations/warscapes-conversation-shobasakthi.

Silva, Neluka, ed. (2002) *The Hybrid Island* (London: Zed).

Sivanandan, A. (1981) *A Different Hunger* (London: Pluto).

_____. (1984) 'Sri Lanka: Racism and the Politics of Underdevelopment', *Race & Class* 26 (1): 1-39.

Sivanesan, Sumugan, 'Alex & I: In Proximity to the Other of Politics', *Law Text Culture*, 17: 129–42.

Smiley, Tavis (2009) Interview with M.I.A. *Tavis Smiley*. PBS, 28 January. pbs.org/wnet/tavissmiley/interviews/hip-hop-artist-m-i-a/.

Spencer, Jonathan, Jonathan Goodhand, Shahul Hasbullah, Bart Klem, Benedikt Korf & Kalinga Tudor Silva. (2015) *Checkpoint, Temple, Church and Mosque: A Collaborative Ethnography of War and Peace* (London: Pluto Press).

Spivak, Gayatri (1988) 'Can the Subaltern Speak?' In *Marxism and the Interpretation of Culture*, Cary Nelson & Lawrence Grossberg, eds. (Urbana: University of Illinois Press), 271–313.

_____. (1996) 'Transnationality and Multiculturalist Ideology', Interview with Deepika Bahri and Mary Vasudeva, in *Between the Lines: South Asians and Postcoloniality*, D. Bahri & M. Vasudeva, eds. (Philadelphia: Temple University Press) 64–89.

_____. (2004) 'Terror: A Speech After 9/11', *Boundary 2*, 31 (2): 81–111.

Sullivan, Tim & Raf Casert (2000) 'For a Pair of African Stowaways, Only Europe Held Hope of a Future', *Los Angeles Times*, 19 March. articles.latimes.com/2000/mar/19/news/mn-10355.

Stratton, Jon (2009) ' "Welcome to paradise": Asylum Seekers, Neoliberalism, Nostalgia and Lucky Miles', *Continuum: Journal of Media and Cultural Studies* 23 (5): 629–45.

Subramanian, Samanth (2014) *Divided Island* (New Delhi: Penguin).

Sydney Morning Herald (2001) ' "Where's the Bus?" Ask Illegal Sri Lankans', *Sydney Morning Herald*, 20 April.

Sumathy, Sivamohan (2001) *Militants, Militarism and the Crisis of (Tamil) Nationalism* (Colombo: Marga Institute).

DOI: 10.1057/9781137444646.0014

_____. (2004) 'The Rise of Militant Tamil Nationalism, Its Assumptions and the Cultural Production of Tamil Women' in *Sri Lankan Society in an Era of Globalization: Struggling To Create A New Social Order*, S.H. Hasbullah & Barrie M. Harrison, eds. (London: Sage), 126–149.

_____. (2014) 'Surveillance and Survival', *Frontline*, 5 February. http://www.frontline.in/arts-and-culture/cinema/surveillance-and-survival/article5652190.ece.

_____. (forthcoming) 'A Spoonful of Sugar: The Quest for Survival and Justice in the Violence of Gender and the Violence of Sex in the Politics of the Ethnic Conflict in Sri Lanka'.

Taylor, Diana (1997) *Disappearing Acts* (Durham: Duke University Press).

Thinakkural (2010) 'Editorial', translation from *Groundviews*, 19 September. groundviews.org/2010/09/23/translation-of-tamil-newspaper-reports-on-the-lessons-learnt-reconciliation-commission-hearings-held-in-killinochchi-and-mullaitivu/.

Thomson-Senanayake, Jane (2014) A Sociological Exploration of Disappearance in Sri Lanka (Hong Kong: Asian Human Rights Commission).

United Nations (2010) 'Deeming Sri Lanka Execution Video Authentic, UN Expert Calls for War Crimes Probe" *UN News Centre*, 7 January, accessed 15 May 2010. un.org/apps/news/story.asp?NewsID=33423&Cr=sri+lanka&Cr1/.

_____. (2011) 'Report of the Secretary-General's Panel of Experts on Accountability in Sri Lanka', *UN.org*, 31 March, accessed 30 July 2014. un.org/News/dh/infocus/Sri_Lanka/POE_Report_Full.pdf.

_____.(2012) 'Report of the Secretary-General's Internal Review Panel on United Nations Action in Sri Lanka', *UN.org*, accessed 30 June 2014. http://www.un.org/News/dh/infocus/Sri_Lanka/The_Internal_Review_Panel_report_on_Sri_Lanka.pdf.

UNITAR (United Nations Institute for Training and Research) (2011) 'UNOSAT Brief Satellite Applications for Human Security', *UNITAR*. http://www.unitar.org/sites/default/files/UNOSAT_Brief_Sat_App_for_Human_Sec_2011.pdf.

University Teachers for Human Rights (Jaffna) [UTHR (J)] (2009) 'Special Report No. 34', *Let Them Speak: Truth about Sri Lanka's Victims of War*, 13 December, accessed 7 November 2014. uthr.org/SpecialReports/Special%20rep34/Uthr-sp.rp34.htm/.

Visweswaran, Kamala (2012) 'Occupier/ Occupied', *Identities: Global Studies in Culture and Power* 19 (4): 440–51.

DOI: 10.1057/9781137444646.0014

Weiss, Gordon (2011) *The Cage* (London: Bodley Head).

Weizman, Eyal (2011) *The Least of All Possible Evils* (London: Verso).

_____.& Zachary Manfredi (2013) ' "From Figure to Ground": A Conversation with Eyal Weizman on the Politics of *The Humanitarian Present*', *Qui Parle*, 22 (1): 167–92.

Welikala, Asanga, ed. (2012) *The Sri Lankan Republic at 40: Reflections on Constitutional History, Theory and Practice* (Colombo: Centre for Policy Alternatives).

Wickremesekera, Channa (2012) *In the Same Boat* (Colombo: Perera-Hussein).

Wijeyeratne, Roshan de Silva (2012) 'Republican Constitutionalism and Sinhalese Buddhist Nationalism in Sri Lanka: Towards an Ontological Account of the Sri Lankan State' in *The Sri Lankan Republic at 40: Reflections on Constitutional History, Theory and Practice*, Asanga Welikala, ed. (Colombo: Centre for Policy Alternatives) 403–40.

Williams, Randall (2010) *The Divided World* (Minneapolis: University of Minnesota Press).

Williams, Robert W. (2003) 'Terrorism, Anti-terrorism and the Normative Boundaries of the U.S. Polity: The Spatiality of Politics after 11 September 2001', *Space and Polity*, 7 (3): 273–92.

Wood, Elizabeth Jean (2009) 'Armed Groups and Sexual Violence: When Is Wartime Rape Rare?' *Politics & Society*, 37 (1): 131–62.

Young, Robert (2009) 'The Violent State', *Naked Punch* (Lahore), 02, October 16. nakedpunch.com/articles/38.

Filmography

Arnestad, Beate (2007) *My Daughter, The Terrorist* (Norway: Morten Daae).

Macrae, Callum (2012) *Sri Lanka's Killing Fields* (Channel Four, UK).

_____.(2014) *No Fire Zone* (Outsider Films, UK).

Rowland, Michael James (2007) *Lucky Miles* (Australia: Madman)

DOI: 10.1057/9781137444646.0014

Index

DOI: 10.1057/9781137444646.0015

DOI: 10.1057/9781137444646.0015

9 781137 444639